THE UNIVERSITY OF
WINCHESTER

THE IDEA
— OF THE —
REPUBLIC

Norberto Bobbio
— and —
Maurizio Viroli

Translated by Allan Cameron

polity

Copyright © this translation Polity Press 2003

First published in Italian as *Dialogo intorno alla repubblica* © Giuseppe Laterza & Figli 2001, Rome–Bari.

English language edition arranged through the mediation of Eulama Literary Agency.
Published with the financial assistance of the Italian Ministry of Foreign Affairs.

First published in 2003 by Polity Press in association with Blackwell Publishing Ltd

Editorial office:
Polity Press
65 Bridge Street
Cambridge CB2 1UR, UK

Marketing and production:
Blackwell Publishing Ltd
108 Cowley Road
Oxford OX4 1JF, UK

Distributed in the USA by
Blackwell Publishing Inc.
350 Main Street
Malden, MA 02148, USA

A catalogue record for this book is available from the British Library.

Library of Congress Cataloging-in-Publication Data

Bobbio, Norberto, 1909-
[Dialogo intorno alla repubblica. English]
The idea of the republic / Norberto Bobbio and Maurizio Viroli; translated by
    Allan Cameron.
    p. cm.
"First published in Italian as Dialogo intorno alla repubblica"-T.p. verso.
ISBN 0-7456-3096-0 (hb: alk. paper) – ISBN 0-7456-3097-9 (pb: alk. paper)
1. State, The. I. Viroli, Maurizio. II. Title.
JC131 .B63 2003
320' .01-dc21   2002155687

Typeset in 11 on 13 pt Berling
by Kolam Information Services Pvt. Ltd, Pondicherry, India.
Printed and bound in Great Britain by MPG Books Ltd, Bodmin, Cornwall

For further information on Polity, visit our website: www.polity.co.uk

Contents

Introduction to the English Edition

In presenting this work to an English-speaking readership, it seems only right to ascertain whether the observations that Norberto Bobbio and I made in the Italian original have turned out to be well-founded. Personally, I feel that many of the points raised have proved to be even more relevant today than when the book was first published in the spring of 2001.

I refer primarily to the political ideal of the republic. As the reader will discover, Bobbio and I discuss at length the value and topicality of the classical ideal of a republic understood as a political constitution based on the principle of the common good. It is my opinion that this ideal retains all its usefulness to the current political situation in Europe, particularly as a bulwark against the worrying populist trends that are undermining democratic regimes to varying degrees.

The most significant example is that of the French elections in 2002. When faced with Jean-Marie Le Pen, a xenophobic and populist candidate, the citizens of France were able to avoid the danger he posed by rediscovering the Republic's values, which rose above party loyalty and private interests. Unfortunately, at other times in the history of the twentieth century, democratic, socialist and liberal forces did not know how to achieve a similar republican unity and they opened the way to the rise of populist demagogues who generate enthusiastic followings and create consensus by pandering to the people's worst instincts – the worst of all being nationalism. Populist demagogues cannot be defeated in the name of a single class or just part of the people. They can only be defeated in the name of wider political principles, such as the principles of the republic, the most important of which is the common good.

Republican political theory, which was reborn as a subject for historical and theoretical studies in English and American universities, seems to have become a reference point in European political battles. The ideals of republicanism are in fact an alternative to the right's cultural models. Whereas political movements and parties of the right invoke the idea of liberty as the absence of impediments to individual action, supporters of republicanism proclaim that true political freedom is emancipation from forms of domination or, in other words, emancipation from dependency on the arbitrary will of other individuals. The right perceives laws as a restriction on freedom; republicanism perceives them as freedom's most necessary foundation. It is always difficult to make sensible predictions about political events, but it may be that the conflict between right and left will in the coming years become a conflict between two different perceptions of liberty and no longer between exponents of freedom and exponents of equality. One freedom will be freedom from regulations and the law, and the other freedom emancipation from forms of domination. Unfortunately many leaders of the European left coming from a socialist or communist background are still very diffident towards the republican tradition, and by so being they deprive themselves of the chance to respond effectively to the right's cultural and political initiatives. They fail to realize that the much sought-after third way between liberalism and socialism has always existed and it is called republicanism.

Introduction

In our dialogue, Bobbio and I expressed our concerns over political life in democratic societies. Money has an increasingly fundamental role in determining the outcomes of elections. Personal parties have appeared and achieved great successes, and as Bobbio explains, such parties are in fact created by one person in contrast with parties in the proper sense of the term, which by definition are made up of an association of persons. The power of money and personal parties are not something new to democracy, but they are both particularly dangerous in the current situation, whose distinguishing features are the decline of the great ideologies, the absence of political leaders who can excite and strengthen civic fervour and the decline in the role of political parties as training grounds for democratic awareness. When we wrote our dialogue, there was no sign of political leaders, forces or movements capable of checking the domination of money and defeating the personal parties. It does not appear that the situation has improved, at least not in Italy.

The danger threatening European democracies is once again nationalism, the ideology that claims that the principle of the state is to protect the unity of the nation or people from contamination by extraneous cultural, religious or ethnic elements, or from the assimilation of the national culture within other cultures. Nationalist leaders, with differing emphases from one country to another, are equally hostile to the transformation of national societies into societies in which different cultures and religions coexist with the same civil, political and social rights and to the process of European integration. They promote discriminatory policies in place of religious and cultural pluralism, and they insist on strengthening regional and local autonomy in place of European integration.

It is my belief that the most effective response to nationalism both intellectually and politically is not cosmopolitanism, which asserts that we must consider ourselves and others to be citizens of the world with the same fundamental rights and teaches us that our national identity is no more than an accident of birth, which may have some small emotional significance but nothing more, and that identity must give way to universal principles dictated by reason. Nor is it the constitutional patriotism that asserts that our patriotism as citizens must be loyalty to the democratic constitution and its principles of freedom and equality. Rather it is the old tradition of republican patriotism which aims to promote loyalty to the republic amongst citizens, where 'republic' is understood as a collection of political and cultural values. As I try to explain in this dialogue, republican patriotism does not teach diffidence towards other cultures and neither does it make people deaf to appeals for solidarity from other peoples. Here again the French example can be of assistance: they did not invoke the universal principles of cosmopolitanism or constitutional patriotism against Le Pen's nationalism. They appealed to the ideal of the *République*, which of course includes the constitution but is also a particular history and a particular culture. They did not proclaim themselves to be citizens of the world, but to be French in the best sense of the word and in relation to their history and cultural tradition.

The question of nationalism raises the religious question. As the reader will be able to discover, Bobbio is more inclined than I am to express his appreciation of religious faith and to believe that over the centuries the love of God (and not the fear of God) has motivated men and women to carry out charitable works to assist the suffering. Yet when I reread some passages now, they have a prophetic quality to them. Bobbio warns us against the immense destructive power of religion. He argues that the nineteenth century

> was dominated by the idea that religion was the opiate of the people. Is there still anyone who has the courage to argue this view? It may not be the opiate of the people, but it could be something even more dangerous: the drug of the people. An opiate puts you to sleep, but drugs can kill.

Introduction

Look at what is happening in the conflict between Palestinians and Jews, as a result of religious extremists on both sides. Every time you get close to a solution, the extremists kill. Religion often leads to crime. The young man who killed Rabin said, 'God ordered me to do it'. This is sufficient to demonstrate that religion is not the opiate of the people, but very possibly something worse.

Unfortunately the terrorist attacks on 11 September 2001 and the worsening situation in the Israeli–Palestinian conflict demonstrate Bobbio's clarity of vision.

However paradoxical it might appear, I believe that only one religion could avert the threat of religious fundamentalism to democracy, and that would be a civic religion that strengthened the citizens' loyalty to democratic institutions. Only such a religion could engender the necessary moral strength to resist terrorist attacks. Military, economic and technological power is not sufficient to defeat an enemy capable of giving meaning and beauty to sacrificing one's life, if citizens of the democracies do not have the inner strength to make sacrifices in defence of their common freedoms. Only a civic religion can provide that inner strength.

Unfortunately the democracies appear to have exhausted their capacity to keep that civic religion alive, a development to which both Bobbio and I give great prominence. No political leaders are emerging, and still less ones capable of exciting strong emotions. Referring to an important study by Guido Dorso, Bobbio stresses that, in spite of such studies, the formation of a great political elite remains a mystery. I believe that here again he has clearly understood the situation. I think, however, that political theory could help the formation of a new democratic elite, if intellectuals were more involved in the business of civic education through their writings and by the example of the way they live, as Norberto Bobbio has done for more than fifty years. In this dialogue, Bobbio provides us with a masterly lesson in intellectual integrity

Introduction

and civic fervour. But if there are no other intellectuals capable of following his example, it will be very difficult to recreate a democratic political elite.

In Italy, this book stirred up bitter controversy over our views on the current Prime Minister of Italy, Silvio Berlusconi (but when we wrote this work, he was the leader of the opposition and the centre-left was in power). Readers can judge for themselves whether there is any justification for our belief that Berlusconi created a party to destroy the Republic founded in 1946. The fact remains that, not content with amending the constitution to allow the return of the descendants of former kings to Italy (without requiring them to renounce their dynastic claims), Berlusconi and his allies then announced their intention to proceed with a reform to make Italy a presidential republic and thus achieve a complete institutional break with the Republic created in 1946.

The success of Berlusconi's political career is something unprecedented in the history of democracies, and could have consequences for other democratic countries. Berlusconi, as I have already pointed out, is the leader of a personal party. He has personal wealth that is infinitely greater than that of democratic leaders in the past. He controls a television and publishing empire. Given the hardly contestable fact that the current Italian Prime Minister has concentrated in his hands greater power than any other politician has had in a democracy, he can profoundly change the way in which consensus is formed. Many commentators do not see anything wrong in all this, while others who are more aware of long-established liberal concerns over the concentration of power (whoever holds that power, even if it were the people), wisely express deep reservations. Bobbio and I are amongst this second group.

In spite of the controversies over its political content, this book created a great deal of interest amongst readers, particularly the young, because of its reflections on the great themes of wisdom in the way we live: religious experience, intransigence and meekness, a sense of duty, the nature of moral assessment and a sense of human history. We have attempted to give some replies to difficult questions on human experience. Whatever opinions they may form about Bobbio's arguments and mine, I hope that readers will appreciate the fact that this short book contains a genuine dialogue motivated by a desire not to win an argument but to seek out truths together. When faced with the dominance of demagogues who seduce the crowd that listens and applauds, and with politics that has been reduced to soundbites and personal attacks, it would be no bad thing if we remembered that democracy primarily means being able to listen and being willing to enter into a dialogue.

Maurizio Viroli

— 1 —

Virtue and the Republic

VIROLI: Some political theorists argue that there is a republican tradition of political thought, as distinct from both the liberal and the democratic ones.[1] In the opinion of such scholars, of whom I am one, republican political theory is primarily characterized by the principle of political freedom. Whereas liberalism perceives freedom as an absence of interference and democracy identifies freedom 'in the power to impose rules upon oneself and not to obey rules other than those imposed on oneself' (these are your own words), republicanism considers true freedom to be the absence of any dependency on the arbitrary will of a single man or a group of men. An obvious example is that of a slave, who may suffer neither oppression nor interference, but is still not free, because he or she is dependent on the arbitrary will of another person. Do you believe that we can speak of republican theory and republican political traditions that are distinct from the democratic and liberal ones?

BOBBIO: I have never encountered republicanism or the republic in my experience as a scholar of political thought. I know little or nothing about the theoreticians of republicanism who have inspired you. Let us look at the facts: there is no entry under 'republicanism' in the very detailed index and summary of a recently published collection of my writings that runs to about 700 pages.[2] I am very sorry to have to tell you that there is not even an entry for 'republic', which is truly surprising. Some years ago, I published an article, 'Rule of law or rule of men?' ('Governo delle leggi o governo degli uomini?'), in which I outlined the history of this question starting from the differences between Aristotle, who was an exponent of the former, and Plato, who was an exponent of the latter. I then briefly describe the various categories of the better-known forms of government by men. The 'republic' does not appear anywhere.

As I have told you on other occasions, in my opinion and in that of the great majority of those who have studied politics and law starting with our very own Machiavelli, 'republic' is the name of the form of government that contrasts with 'monarchy' or 'principality'. As you very well know, we only have to think of all the debates over the difference between democratic republics and aristocratic ones, and over the superiority of one over the other, which even involved Montesquieu, one of your preferred authors. However, neither of these resembles the republic of republicans, as you acknowledge yourself.

The republic is an ideal form of state founded on the virtues and patriotism of its citizens. Virtue and patriotism were Jacobin ideals, to which terror was then added. In reality, the republic needs terror. You recall the famous speech by Robespierre on virtue and terror. In my opinion, the republic is an ideal state that does not exist anywhere. It is a rhetorical ideal, and it is therefore difficult for me to understand what you mean by republic and republicans. We won't mention the Italian Republic.

Res publica can be used as a general term for a state, any state. There is no problem here: Jean Bodin's famous work, *De la République*, appears in Italian translation as *Dello Stato* (*Concerning the State*), and it distinguishes and describes a variety of forms of government, names the three classical ones of monarchy, aristocracy and democracy, which are all equally *républiques* or *res publicae*.

V.   The most important meaning of 'republic' is the classical one attributed to it by Cicero, who wrote that *res publica* means 'that which belongs to the people' ('res publica res populi'), and added that a people is not just any mass of persons gathered together, but rather an organized society that is founded on the observance of justice and common interest. This concept of republic, which is clearly very different from Bodin's in that it excludes absolute power, is also adopted by Rousseau when he writes: 'I therefore give the name of "Republic" to every state that is governed by laws, no matter what the form of its administration may be: for only in such a case does the public interest govern, and the *res publica* rank as a reality.'[3]

But let's put definitions to one side. I would like to point out my surprise at hearing you say that you never came across republicanism or the republic during your formation as a political thinker. The reason for my surprise is that Carlo Cattaneo, an important figure in the republican pantheon, holds a prominent place in your intellectual history. It was Cattaneo who wrote that 'freedom is the republic' and it was Cattaneo who emphasized that the Italian medieval republics had to be credited with 'having instilled in the lowliest plebeian a sense of legality and civic dignity', thus surpassing ancient Athens, 'whose noble citizenship always had a lower layer of slavery'.[4]

B.   I did not see Cattaneo in terms of the concept of republic; I approached him through his federalism, the concept for which he became famous. In other words, I was struck by his federalist concept of a republic as opposed to Mazzini's unitary one. Mazzini was horrified by this idea of the republic as a federation of tiny republics, which would have taken Italy back to the time of the medieval city-republics (*comuni*), so admired by Bossi.[5] I have never looked on Cattaneo as a republican political writer. To be frank, the idea of republic is so small a part of my thinking and the way I categorize my conceptual system that for me Cattaneo is not a republican but the federalist of the Risorgimento, who then expanded his idea of federalism to Europe.

V.   I agree, but if we put Cattaneo in the framework of our debate, we have to acknowledge that there are at least two versions of republicanism, the unitary one and the federalist one.

B.   It seems to me that the republic of republicans, of which you are one, is a form of ideal state, a 'moral paragon', as Montesquieu's republic has been called, and his republic influenced the French revolutionaries. It is an ideal state that exists nowhere, or exists only in the writings of the authors you quote, who are so heterogeneous that it is difficult to find their common denominator. They include Livy, Mazzini, Cattaneo and who knows how many medieval and modern writers. Some of these were genuinely political writers and historians who, like Machiavelli, wrote commentaries on Roman history, which was perceived as a model history. They were discussing the state as it should be and not as it is. These were either dreams of an ideal future or nostalgia for an ideal past.

V.   I grant you that without any difficulty. Supposing that the republic of republicans is a moral ideal, could it perhaps be the case that it is an important moral and political ideal in a period like ours that is so short of political ideals capable of sustaining civil commitment and acting as a reference point for political action?

B.   This is the same argument that we have discussed on several occasions in relation to your book *From Politics to the Reason of State*.[6] In politics I am a realist. You can only talk politics if you keep a clinical eye firmly on history. Whether it is monarchical or republican, politics is the struggle for power. To talk of ideals, as you do, is in my mind to engage in rhetoric. Even when your writers of great renown spoke of republics, politics was what was actually happening on the ground, as it always has been since the times of the Greeks. I can understand politics as the struggle for power, but if you speak of politics whose goal is a republic based on the virtue of its citizens, then I wonder what exactly this citizens' virtue is supposed to be. Tell me where you can find a state that is founded on the virtue of its citizens and does not have recourse to the use of force! The definition of the state that continuously recurs is the one whereby the state holds a monopoly on the *legitimate* use of force, and that force is necessary because the majority of the citizens are not virtuous but corrupt. That is why the state needs to use force, and that is my concept of politics. This type of politics differs from the politics of those who feel they can speak of states founded on the virtue of their citizens. As I have said, virtue is a Jacobin ideal. The reason for having states, including republics, is to curb immoral citizens, who constitute the majority. No real state is founded on the virtue of its citizens. Real states are governed by a written or unwritten constitution that establishes the rules of behaviour precisely on the assumption that its citizens are not generally virtuous.

V.   You explained the nature of civil virtue and the reason why it is necessary in republics when you said that the purpose of states 'is to curb its immoral citizens'. Precisely because the main purpose of states is to check the arrogant, the ambitious and the corrupt, citizens have to be able 'to keep a firm grip on freedom' and to desire it too, as Cattaneo wrote quoting Machiavelli.

B.   I too have quoted that passage from Machiavelli many times![7]

V.   The meaning of that passage is that to keep a check on the corrupt you need not only good laws but also citizens who are distinguished by civic virtue. My republicans and your mentors are in agreement. Machiavelli and Cattaneo come together on this point: if you do not have citizens who are willing to be vigilant, committed and capable of resisting the arrogant and serving the public good, the republic dies and it becomes a place in which a few dominate and the others are subject to them.

B.   In one of the first articles published after the Liberation in the Action Party's newspaper, *Giustizia e Libertà*, I wrote that democracy needs good laws and good behaviour. What is good behaviour if not what you in an overly rhetorical manner call 'virtue'?[8]

V.   Of course, civic virtue is not, in my opinion, the desire to sacrifice oneself for the fatherland. It is a civic virtue for men and women to wish to live in dignity and, as they know that you cannot live in dignity within a corrupt community, they do what they can, when they can, to assist the common freedom. They carry out their professional activities without unlawful advantage and without profiting from the need or weakness of others. They lead a family life based on mutual respect, so that their home resembles a small republic rather than a monarchy or a group of strangers held together by self-interest or the television. They fulfil their civic duties, but they are by no means subservient; they are capable of mobilizing themselves to prevent the approval of an unjust law or to force those in power to deal with matters of common interest. They are active in various kinds of associations (professional, sporting, cultural, political and religious). They follow national and international political developments, and they want to understand but not be led or indoctrinated. They wish to know and discuss the republic's history and reflect upon its historical memory.

For some, the principal reason for this commitment arises from a sense of morality, or more specifically from their indignation over discrimination, corruption, arrogance, vulgarity and the abuse of office. In others there prevails an aesthetic desire for decency and propriety. Still others are motivated by legitimate interests, such as the desire for safe roads, pleasant parks, well-maintained squares, monuments that haven't been vandalized, proficient schools and proper hospitals. Indeed some become committed because they want to be respected, receive public accolades, sit at the top table, speak in public and be first in line at ceremonies. In many cases, these motives operate together, and one strengthens the other.

This type of civic virtue is not impossible. We could all think of many people who respond to this description of the citizen who has a sense of civic responsibility and who have only done good for their communities and themselves.

B.   To speak of civic virtue is important in order to resist the indifference and political apathy that unfortunately now prevail in our country for reasons that are quite understandable and need not be repeated here. In the period following the Liberation, there was enthusiasm and a desire to become involved as a reaction to the policies that were imposed from above under fascism. Everyone gave their own contribution. There is a need for good moral standards and a virtuous citizenry.

— 2 —

Patriotism

V.   Civic virtue: this is the real meaning of the republican ideal of patriotism.

B.   Be careful with patriotism. Remember the motto 'Dulce et decorum est pro patria mori', which used to be repeated endlessly and engraved above the doors of public buildings. Fascism also spoke of the fatherland; it said that you had to defend the fatherland and give your life for the fatherland. The word 'fatherland' lends itself to the deceptions used by those who hold power. If you think about it properly, this certainly is a republican motto, but who exploits a motto of this kind? Who are the people that utter this motto? Often tyrants and petty despots.

V.   You are right. The word I find most misleading in that motto is *dulce* – 'sweet'. I do not understand how dying, even for the fatherland, can ever be described as 'sweet'. It could be described as 'necessary', 'glorious' or 'heroic', but never sweet.

B.   'Sweet' is an added consolation, like saying that the gods favour those who die young. This expression also belongs to that kind of consolatory rhetoric.

V.   We will discuss rhetoric later, but for the moment let's stick with the question of patriotism. You proclaim yourself to be a European and a citizen of the world, and yet you are more Piedmontese than anyone else; I proclaim myself to be a patriot, but live much of my time abroad and am constantly on the move. Don't you find that odd?

B.   I fully accept that I have always been a provincial. You know what they call people from Turin? *Bogianen*. This means that they never go anywhere and always stay in their own little hole. It is the opposite of a globe-trotter. I am a *bogianen*, and you are a globe-trotter.

V.   In *Liberal Socialism*, Carlo Rosselli emphasized that the socialist insistence on ignoring 'the highest values of national life' was a terrible mistake in terms of both ideals and politics. Even if they did this to combat 'primitive, degenerate or selfish forms of attachment to one's country', their policy ended up 'making it easier for other movements that exploited the myth of the nation to build their political fortunes'.[1] According to Rosselli, socialists had not understood that 'national sentiment' was not an artificial construct, but a genuine human passion, particularly for those peoples who had gained their independence late. Instead of attempting to replace national sentiment with internationalism, socialists should have worked to purge national sentiment of any nationalism, idolization of the state or myth of national superiority, and to transform this national sentiment into a constructive political force for European unity.[2] Rosselli established a clear demarcation between patriotism and nationalism. He identified the former with the ideals of liberty based on respect for the rights of other peoples and the latter with expansionist policies pursued by reactionary regimes.[3] Both appeal to national sentiment and both evoke strong feelings; yet precisely because of this they have to be used against each other. Rosselli stressed that, instead of condemning national sentiment as a prejudice, antifascists should have placed patriotism at the very centre of the political programme. He wrote that the antifascist revolution was 'a patriotic duty'.[4] To create their own patriotism, antifascists needed an idea of fatherland that was totally different from the one used by fascist demagogues. He wrote that our fatherland 'is not measured in terms of frontiers and cannons, but coincides with our moral world and with the fatherland of all free men'.[5] This value perfectly agrees with antifascism's other values: human dignity, freedom, justice, culture and labour. Fascists exalt the nation and Italy; antifascists must also present themselves as the defenders of the national and the Italian spirit, but their nation must be a free nation that is open to Europe and the rest of the world. Their Italy must include the better Italy, the Italy of Mazzini, Garibaldi and Pisacane.[6] This Italy of civilized Italians is made up of the peasants, workers and intellectuals who have been able to retain their own dignity. The loyalty of antifascists must only go to this Italy and they should not be afraid of the accusation of being traitors: 'We can be proud of being conscious traitors of the fascist fatherland, because we are loyal to another fatherland.'[7]

B. The fatherland is the place where you came into this world, grew up and received your education. It is a rhetorical argument to say that a despotic state or a state that is not a republic is not your fatherland. Was Italy under fascism still your fatherland or wasn't it? Many people said that they no longer considered fascist Italy to be their fatherland. If you read the diaries of Piero Calamandrei, you will find that he often says that fascism has taken away the idea of fatherland. On 10 August 1943, a few days after the fall of fascism, he wrote:

> One of fascism's greatest crimes was to kill off a sense of
> fatherland. For twenty years, this word 'fatherland' has

filled people with disgust: it was the presumptuous arrogance that could never speak of Italy without adding that
the whole world looked to Rome; it was the tone of
threatening authoritarianism worthy of a puppet theatre
that filled the *duce*'s speeches or the radio presenter's
announcements. This use of the word 'fatherland' made
any allusion to patriotism intolerable even for those who
have strong stomachs when it comes to digesting the ob-
noxious. We had the impression that we had been occu-
pied by foreigners: these fascist Italians who encamped on
our land were foreigners, or if they were Italians, then we
were not.[8]

V.   But have you thought about why Calamandrei wrote
that fascism took away our idea of fatherland? He could
only have said that because for him fatherland does not
mean the place in which we are born, which no one can
take away, but rather only the *polis* in which everyone can
live freely and therefore not feel foreign. Besides, the idea
of being a foreigner in one's own country often recurs in
your own writings; indeed you have said on many occasions that you were ashamed of being Italian. Clearly it is
not enough to be born in a place to feel that that place is
your fatherland.

B.   There is an ideal fatherland that does not coincide
with a specific territory.

V.   The Romans used two different terms: *patria* and
natio; *patria* meant the *res publica* or politic constitution,
the laws and the resulting way of life (and therefore also
the culture); *natio* meant the place of birth and all that was
linked to the place, such as ethnic identity and language.

B.   At the beginning of his *Divine Comedy*, Dante states
that he is 'Florentina natione, non moribus'. I too have said
that I am Italian by nation but not by moral behaviour. I
think of myself as anti-Italian in the sense that I feel
different from the mass of Italians. There is the anti-Italian

and the arch-Italian. The fascists were arch-Italians, while antifascists did not consider themselves Italians in the same manner. Fascists belonged to the other Italy. I remember Gobetti's famous statement: 'For some time I have realized that Gentile belongs to the other Italy.'[9] This concept of the two Italies could be used to develop the distinction between fatherland and nation.

V.   Perhaps it would help to return once again to Cattaneo, who correctly believed that the history of Italy in its most essential aspects was driving towards the creation of a federal republic, 'but this is a feature of our nation, whose republican spirit can be encountered in all its classes..., and it appears that our nation cannot achieve great things without this form of government'.[10] It seems to me that this passage shows us that there has always been an Italy that aspires to civic principles, alongside the other Italy which I would call the Italy of the arrogant and the servile, an Italy that belongs to those who admire the strong, those who are always ready to serve the powerful and those who are masters of the art of flattery. This is not the Italy of which Cattaneo speaks. Both Italies are part of our history and of our present.

B.   When Gian Enrico Rusconi insisted upon the importance of the concept of nation,[11] I would tell him that the concept of nation is very vague, but I never suggested the concept of fatherland in its place. I told him that if we look at history, we find that there are many Italies. There is the Italy of the educated and the Italy of those who are born with few opportunities; there is the Italy that is obsessed with who wins the football league and those capable of violence over a football match; and there is the Italy of the heroes of the Risorgimento and those who fought for national unification. There are Italians who are proud of their history: not the political, social or religious history of Italy, but the literary and artistic history that includes Dante, Petrarch, and the great painters of the Renaissance – those who contributed in some way to the formation of European culture. That is my Italy, the Italy that I identify with, and the Italy that makes me proud to be Italian. When they wanted to demonstrate their loyalty to Italy in Trento, they erected a monument to Dante. This is the elite Italy. The majority of people know nothing about it. It is the Italy that keeps up the tradition of the great poets, with such names as Leopardi, Foscolo, and Manzoni, and ends with Giuseppe Verdi.

V. Verdi? I am happy to hear that. Verdi is a great symbol for those of us who are patriotic.

B. The first opera I ever saw was *La traviata* when I was taken by my parents as a child of ten or eleven years, after the First World War. I never forgot it. I was completely enchanted. I can even remember the name of the tenor who took the part of Alfredo. I think it was Dolci (although I cannot recall his Christian name). My fondness for Verdi may depend on precisely the fact that *La traviata* was the first opera I ever went to. I know that opera off by heart, and I particularly love the first act. I must confess that it irritates me a bit when in the second act I hear the father Germont coming out with that 'Di Provenza il mare e il suol' and, even worse, that 'Pura siccome un angelo / Iddio mi dié una figlia: / se Alfredo nega riedere / in seno alla famiglia' and so on. But I never forget the beautiful, sublime and heart-breaking aria in the last act 'Addio, del passato'. These are just a few notes. As a dilettante I can find no explanation, and I wish some expert could tell me why they have such an extraordinary power of expression. Verdi belongs to the Italy that I identify with. On my mother's side I came from a family of music lovers, and when as a boy after the First World War I started to become interested in music, Wagner and not Verdi was all the rage in the opera houses. However, my friend and fellow student at university, Massimo Mila, who was to become one of the most famous musicologists in Italy, wrote a graduation thesis on the opera of Giuseppe Verdi, which was immediately published by Laterza in 1933 on the advice of Benedetto Croce (Mila was twenty-three at the time). Our love for the great composer was part of our emotional development. Since then I have always considered Verdi to be one of the highest and noblest expressions of our national genius. Just think about it: there were more than forty years between the austere and awe-inspiring chorus in *Nabucco*, which was written when the composer was not even thirty years old (1842), and the song of an inconsolable Othello over Desdemona's body (1887). In the intervening period of almost a half-century there was an endless number of beautiful arias expressing love, anger and death scenes, and there were innumerable choruses and scores for dances. I love *Don Carlo* (1883), the only opera that I went to see on the first night at La Scala and then listened to again and again on a CD. On one occasion when I was in Buenos Aires amongst music-loving friends who were giving a party for me, I raised my glass and began to sing: 'Bevi, bevi, bevi . . . Bevi con me' (Iago, *Otello*).

V. Apart from Verdi and the great artists and scientists of the past, I believe that our identity is also to be found in the squares, streets, public buildings and monuments that in many of our cities recall struggles to gain freedom or episodes in which we experienced liberty and self-government. Palazzo Vecchio in Florence, Piazza del Campo in Siena with its Palazzo Pubblico, monuments to commemorate Garibaldi and Mazzini and the small plaques that remember the martyrs of the Resistance all have great personal significance. To me they represent a strong and honourable Italy.

B. Of course, the Palazzo Pubblico in Siena has Lorenzetti's fresco depicting good government. I lived in Siena for two years. Lorenzetti's fresco inspired a paper I wrote on good government, which I read to the Accademia dei

Lincei on 20 June 1981 in the presence of the then President of the Italian Republic, Sandro Pertini, who I consider to be one of the very few representatives of good government during the period of our First Republic. Moreover, I need hardly remind you that Quentin Skinner has written an article on that fresco's literary and figurative sources.[12]

V. Italian thinkers have also made fundamental contributions to the history of political thought. I am not only referring to Machiavelli for whom I have such admiration. On this point, you only have to consider the legal and political theory of the free city that was formulated by fourteenth-century jurists and political philosophers. It is true that in the seventeenth and eighteenth centuries, the centres of political thought are to be found elsewhere: in the England of Hobbes and Locke and the France of Montesquieu and the encyclopaedists. Yet our political thought had in the preceding centuries created the modern idea of a republic understood as a free community of citizens who live under the rule of law. This is a very rich intellectual tradition, but one that we have not nurtured as much as it deserves. We could and should have done more.

B. With the exception of Machiavelli, my authors have not been Italian. I have mainly studied Hobbes, Locke, Kant and Rousseau.

V. What about Cattaneo and Rosselli, on whom you have written so much?[13]

B. But I never made them the subject of the courses I taught. I have never claimed that there is anything that unites my intellectual activities. I became involved with Hobbes and Cattaneo, but this was the result of various contingencies. When I became interested in Cattaneo, I did so because with the end of fascism we had to prepare for what came after. The only author in the Italian tradition who fascism had never managed to tarnish was Cattaneo. The encounter with Hobbes was pure chance: Luigi Firpo had founded a series published by UTET called 'Classics of Political Thought' and he asked me to edit *De Cive*. Hobbes is an author I find extremely attractive because of his intellectual power and his style.

V.   I knew it; Hobbes was the 'false mentor' who instilled in you this acrimonious attitude to rhetoric. Hobbes detested eloquence, if by eloquence we mean the ability to persuade people not only by appealing to their reason, but also to their emotions.

B.   You only have to consider the chapter on the causes of the disintegration of the state, in which Hobbes narrates the myth of Medea, the sorceress who symbolized eloquence and persuaded the daughters of Pelias, the King of Thessaly, to cut their ageing father up (a metaphor for civil war) and boil him in the insane hope of restoring the vigour of his youth. You have to admit that it is a wonderful passage.

V.   The problem is that, under the influence of Hobbes, you have come to loathe eloquence and rhetoric. However you have also expressed your admiration for the militant philosopher. As well as engaging in the critical analysis of concepts and problems, the militant philosopher needs to persuade his or her fellow citizens to take action; he has to arouse people's indignation and exhort them to stand up for themselves. To do all this, he must also work on their emotions. How can you obtain these results if, when you write or speak, you pay no attention to the persuasive aspects of your argumentation?

B.   These are different aspects of a person's mind. I am both a realist and a man of passions. I am a realist when I examine facts and attempt to interpret actual human conflicts, but I am also an emotional man. I believe there is a definite split within my head between the man of reason and the man of passion. On many occasions I have been both one and the other, possibly in a contradictory manner. I simply don't know. It was passion that made me take part in the Resistance in the final years of fascism and drove me to join Giustizia e Libertà. You are well acquainted with Guttuso's famous sketch of a clandestine meeting of Giustizia e Libertà held in 1939 under fascism.[14] It hangs proudly here on my study wall. I acknowledge that this shows me as a man of passion. Because of this experience, I have always toned down my arguments during the many years I was teaching. I never let my students know what my political passions were. I taught with a kind of cold detachment. One of my favourite authors for use in my courses was Kelsen, who avoided value judgements and constructed a juridical system that could be filled with any content. The pure theory of law can be applied to both the United States and the Soviet Union – to totalitarian systems and to democratic ones. My lessons in the philosophy of law were inspired by this schematism. I even became interested in the logic of normative predicates, deontic logic that deals with purely formal relationships between what is prohibited, what is enforced and what is allowed.

V.   Emotion and eloquence, together with reason, have to be kept in a sublime balance. Indeed your Hobbes, who in *De cive* was so fiercely dismissive of eloquence, ended the *Leviathan* with the admission that 'if there be not powerfull Eloquence, which procureth attention and Consent, the effect of Reason would be little'. Ideally wisdom is therefore a mixture of reason and eloquence: analysis is the time for reason and engagement with society is the time for eloquence. Consider the way Hobbes uses a metaphor. Classical works on rhetoric dictate that metaphors should be used as a powerful means for motivating people. Metaphors can demonstrate concepts to readers or listeners in the form of images. When Hobbes writes that states relate to each other like gladiators, he manages to explain the concept of the state of war through the imagination and, because of this, his arguments are particularly persuasive.

B.   My passion for Hobbes is partly based on his use of metaphor. His writings are particularly rich in imagery. I even thought of making a collection of Hobbes's metaphors and studying them. Some of them are truly wonderful and often taken from the theatre or from the science of optics. Besides, the Leviathan, this monster that devours people, is itself a great metaphor. Hobbes also had a poetic bent. He wrote an autobiography in verse (*Vita carmine expressa*), in which he narrates his entire life in Latin couplets. One of the last times I spoke in public, which was in June 1995 at the opening of the International Congress of the Philosophy of Law, of which I was president, I made quite an impression by quoting a line from his verse biography, which ends with 'et iam iacta est vitae longa fabula mea' ('the long story of my life is now over'). He was then over eighty. Hobbes was a poet, but at the same time he had an extraordinary clarity of thought. This is why Hobbes is one of the thinkers I look up to.

V.   Those metaphors which we both like add clarity to his arguments.

B.   Hobbes uses metaphors to show you concepts in such a clear and penetrating manner that you can never forget them.

— 3 —

What Kind of Freedom?

V. Hobbes also developed the idea of freedom understood as the absence of interference, the so-called negative freedom that later became one of the principles of liberal political thought. His concept of liberty as the absence of interference led him to argue that the citizens of a republic such as Lucca were no more free than the subjects of an absolute monarch such as the Sultan of Constantinople, given that both were subject to the law. He chose to ignore that the citizens of Lucca were made freer than the subjects of Constantinople by the fact that in Lucca both the rulers and the citizens were subject to the civil and constitutional laws, whereas in Constantinople the Sultan was above the law and could dispose of the life and property of his subjects as he wished, thus forcing them to live in a state of complete dependency and in the absence of liberty.

Unlike Hobbes, a republican argues that in order to achieve political freedom you need to oppose both interference and coercion in the literal sense of the word, on the one hand, and dependency on the other, because the state of dependency is a constraint upon an individual's will and therefore a violation of his or her liberty. This means that anyone who cares about true individual freedom *has to be a liberal*, but cannot *only* be a liberal. He or she must also be willing to sustain political programmes that aim to reduce the arbitrary powers that force many men and women to live in a state of dependency.

B.   The concept of independence is clear when it refers to states, which are considered to be sovereign. By sovereignty we mean that they do not recognize a higher power ('potestas superiorem non recognoscens'), although the development of an international order means that for some time states have started to acknowledge various limitations on their own sovereignty in order to create a confederation such as the current UN. I find it more difficult to understand what independence means in the sense of 'superiorem non recognoscens', if it is applied to the individuals who make up a state and are subject to its rules. In the tradition of natural law, starting with Hobbes, individuals are sovereign only in the state of nature, and thus they are continuously at war with each other, just as sovereign states are in the international system. In order to save themselves, they have to renounce their own independence, although in the ideal republics they continue to retain it. When you say 'anyone who cares about true individual freedom *has to be a liberal*, but cannot *only* be a liberal', and therefore has to be 'willing to sustain political programmes that aim to reduce the arbitrary powers that force many men and women to live in a state of dependency', I simply do not know what you are talking about.

V.   I think we have a misunderstanding here that we can easily resolve. When I refer to the independence of individuals, I mean the absence of dependency on the *arbitrary* will of other individuals, but not to independence from the laws of the state. Philip Pettit gives the example of women who are subjected to the arbitrary will of their husbands in his book on republicanism.[1] The husband may not oppress the wife, but if he wants to, he can. In other words, being subject to the will of another individual does not mean being oppressed; it means that you *could* be oppressed. As I have said, this is the situation of the slave, who, according to Roman law, is not a slave because he is oppressed, but because he is dependent on his owner's arbitrary will. The problem is that dependency on the arbitrary will of other individuals breeds fear in relation to the persons who possess those arbitrary powers. Fear, in turn, produces a lack of spirit and courage that nurtures servile attitudes and causes people to avert their eyes, to keep silent and to speak only to flatter the powerful. The state of dependency therefore creates an ethos that is wholly incompatible with the mentality of a citizen. This is why it has be contested as the most dangerous enemy of freedom. For republican writers such as Cicero, Sallust, Livy, Machiavelli, Harrington and Rousseau, the opposite of dependency was not the freedom of the state of nature, but dependency on non-arbitrary laws that apply to everyone. In your essay, 'The rule of law or the rule of men?' ['Governo delle leggi o governo degli uomini?'],[2] you wrote that for Cicero freedom meant that everyone was subject to the laws of the republic. As far as I am concerned, the reason why Cicero defines liberty in this manner is that, if the law is understood as a non-arbitrary will that applies to everyone, then the law makes you free by defending you from the arbitrary will of other individuals. I interpret independence in this way, and not as independence from the law.

B.   We can therefore talk of an independent citizen within the state, if he or she is subject solely to the law. There is a wonderful quote from Aristotle, which I use in relation to the superiority of the rule of law over the rule of men; it states that 'the law is without passion'. It lacks passion in the sense that it does not favour one person over another, and it treats everyone in the same manner. Plato, on the other hand, says the opposite: that everyone must be treated according to who he is. On reflection, I am unable to see the difference between independence, the third

meaning of freedom, and the other two meanings of freedom: the absence of interference (negative freedom) and
autonomy (positive freedom). I cannot understand how
freedom understood as independence differs from freedom understood as autonomy. Independence is the ability
to make your own laws. I may be mistaken, but isn't
Selbständigkeit the word used in German for autonomy,
and it actually means 'independence'. We talk of states
being independent and autonomous. It seems to me that
independence and autonomy are synonyms.

V.   I think that dependency and independence refer to a
legal, social and political condition (consider the examples
of a slave, a wife and a subject of an absolute monarch),
whereas autonomy refers to the will or, to use an anti-
quated term, the spirit, and it describes the tendency to
govern one's own behaviour, to rule oneself. You explained this yourself in 1954 when you wrote a clarifica-
tion of the democratic concept of freedom. The example
of a free person, as perceived from a democratic point of
view, is, according to your own writings, a person who has
a free *will*: the 'nonconformist who reasons independently,
speaks his own mind, and does not give in to pressures,
flattery and the dreams of ambition'. In other words, he
has a free will in the sense of self-determination, as opposed to the liberal idea of freedom as *licence* (the absence
of impediment).

The democratic concept of freedom differs from the
liberal concept, because, in the liberal concept, 'freedom
is referred to as something that contrasts with the law, any
form of law, so that every law, whether prohibitive or
imperative, restricts freedom', whereas from a democratic
point of view, freedom is perceived 'as itself a field of
action that conforms with the law; and the distinction is
no longer between an action governed by the law and an
action not governed by the law, but between an action
governed by an autonomous law (or law that is voluntarily
accepted) and an action governed by a heteronomous law

(or law accepted by force)'.[3] In reality, independence and autonomy almost always go hand in hand: a person who lives in a state of juridical independence (is not a slave or serf), political independence (is not a subject of an absolute monarch or despot), or social independence (does not rely on others for his or her maintenance or welfare), is often an autonomous person. In spite of this, I believe that it is possible to distinguish between the three concepts of freedom. The first, which is liberal, asserts that being free means not being subjected to interference; the second, which is republican, asserts that being free (primarily) means not being dependent on the arbitrary will of other individuals; and the third, which is democratic, asserts that being free primarily means being able to decide the rules that govern society.

B.   The real difference between us is my dislike of rhetoric, which in practice I often contradict by my own actions.

V.   I have always told you that, unlike most people, you don't preach what you practise.

B.   I never knew that.

— 4 —

Meekness and Intransigence

V.   Perhaps it is not so much the question of rhetoric that divides us as the question of meekness. You have written a book praising meekness (as opposed to docility, malleability and acquiescence).[1] I, on the other hand, would have written a work in praise of intransigence.

B.   Oh, very good. When we deal with such arguments, we often tend to think of ourselves, and I consider myself to be a meek person, occasionally too meek. I have never been an intransigent person. I have made too many compromises in my life. I have always had friends around me who have been the very model of intransigence, such as Vittorio Foa who very straightforwardly got himself arrested and spent eight years in prison. His *Letters from Prison* were recently published by Einaudi. He never complained and even had little time for Silvio Pellico's *My Prisons*, because he found it too doleful. Gobetti was also intransigent, and he was to some extent the hero of our generation. Gobetti was completely intransigent. Intransigence was one of the words he often used. It meant not giving an inch when fulfilling one's duty to oppose the dictatorship.

V.   I am also thinking of the intransigence of the state – the intransigence in the defence of justice against criminality, corruption and the Mafia, which is the mark of a democratic state. The opposite of intransigence is in this case compromise, or in other words, the tendency to yield, to forgive, to grant amnesties, to absolve and to forget. I believe that intransigence must be one of the founding principles in a republic.

B.   Intransigence is not in the nature of Italians. The intransigent are few and far between; they are an elite. 'If the answer is no, then no it is!', as Mazzini used to say. The intransigent are those people who are willing to sacrifice their own interests for the idea they believe in. Gobetti was a fine example of this. The Italian state is not. I'm not sure whether the state should be as intransigent as you suggest.

I am not entirely in agreement with the arguments of my friend Alessandro Galante Garrone, who has taken a firm stance against the return to Italy of members of the House of Savoy. It is true that the House of Savoy is a dynasty, but responsibility is still personal. Guilt cannot be transmitted from one generation to another. Victor Emmanuel III died in exile, and so did his son Umberto. But what has this to do with the son of the son? I would not be so strict.

V.   I have never argued that in the case of a royal dynasty, the sins of the fathers should be visited upon the sons. What I am saying is that Transitional Regulation XIII, together with Regulation XII which bans the re-establishment of the dissolved Fascist Party, expresses a judgement of great historic and symbolic importance. I see no reason why it should be repealed. If members of the House of Savoy wish to return to Italy, all they need do is renounce their position in line to the throne. If they did this, they would no longer be descendants of the former king, and therefore the regulation would not apply. I would add that it would be dangerous to let the House of Savoy return in the current situation in Italy, with part of northern Italy supporting the separatist Lega Nord[2] and increasing indifference amongst citizens of the Republic.

B. Perhaps what occurred in Turin at the funeral of Edgardo Sogno, an avowed monarchist, is the demonstration of this: it was an apotheosis.[3]

V. Just imagine what would happen if a descendant of a king returns to his homeland and says, 'I am ready to deliver you from the tyranny of the republic, which oppresses you with taxes and does not protect you.'

B. In Piedmont, the ancient monarchical families have not changed. It seems that they were all at the funeral. They have not forgotten. You will not remember, but in the fifties Sogno set up a group called Pace e Libertà ['Peace and Liberty']. It was semi-clandestine and anticommunist – an anticommunism that did not stop at ostracization (famously referred to as *conventio ad excludendum*), but also preached the elimination of communists, including the use of violence. I once told Sogno, who had a certain disliking for me, that I had never been a communist, but I had always thought that, in a democratic state, communists should be fought with democratic arms, as then occurred in Italy, where communists always defended democracy. Communism cannot be fought with coups.

V. Do you see why I place such importance on intransigence? Intransigence means not forgiving and not forgetting too lightly. A lack of intransigence creates spoilt children and not free citizens. Remember that intransigence is perfectly consistent with charity, a value by which I put great store. Real charity is an inner force that requires you to punish (and to reward) in accordance with justice for the public good; it is neither vendetta nor favouritism. But all I hear is talk of forgiveness, amnesty, amnesia, forgetting and pardon. I believe we have forgotten the true meaning of charity. We should educate our young people to the idea that being a citizen requires an inner force that requires you to demand that the republic be intransigent (this is what I attempt to do with my students in Princeton). Yet few trials of those responsible for corruption have reached their conclusion, and very few of the guilty have completed the sentences imposed.

B.   They raised endless objections, and they said the judges were persecuting them. That is Italy for you.

V.   But what is the root of this Italian complaint – this inability to stand firm and be intransigent?

B.   You know this very well, given that you are so well acquainted with the history of Italy. It is an old story, which Guicciardini refers to in his *Ricordi*: 'There are three things I would like to see before I die, but I doubt that I shall see any of them, even if I were to live a long life: to live in a well-ordered republic in our city, Italy freed from all the barbarians and the world delivered from the tyranny of these iniquitous priests.'[4]

V.   I believe that one of the causes is bad religious education. Machiavelli wrote that 'We Italians primarily owe the fact that we have become bad and without religion to the Church and the priests.'[5]

B.   Indeed, there is a problem with bad religious education. It encourages guile, deceit and forms of superstition. It is religion in the shape of superstition and credulity. It is one thing to believe, and quite another to be credulous. A Madonna weeps, and everyone goes to see her. It is the religion of the outer and not the inner world.

— 5 —

Rights and Duties

V.   This inner dimension, this religion of the inner self, is
important because it fosters a sense of duty. You wrote a
book entitled *The Age of Rights*.[1] Shouldn't you follow it
up with an essay on duties? Don't you think that in order
truly to achieve an age of rights, you also need to have a
sense of duty?

B.   The need for rights arises from the need to defend
oneself against oppression, the abuse of power and all
the forms of despotism that we have experienced in our
lifetime. We demanded rights in opposition to the despotism that only demanded duties of its subjects and
acknowledged no rights. Only duties and no rights. We
needed to rebel against the fascist slogan 'Believe, obey
and go to war' ['Credere, obbedire, combattere'], a slogan
that preached blind faith in power and authority. 'You
have no rights; the state is everything. You are called
upon to serve the state and nothing else' – these were
their arguments. Gentile's philosophy, which took Hegel's
theory of the state to its extreme conclusions, argued
that the state is in itself moral because it is superior to
individuals.

V. I understand your reasoning, but if you take rights seriously, you must also take duties seriously: such duties as the duty to defend the freedom of the collectivity and the duty to respect the rights of other individuals. Perhaps we secular thinkers have talked too much of rights and too little of duties.

B. If I had a few more years to live, which I do not, I might be tempted to write *The Age of Duties*. A Charter of the Duties and Responsibilities of States has recently been written as part of a Unesco initiative, and it is to stand alongside the Universal Declaration of Human Rights. I was involved in this initiative by an Italian friend, an ambassador, who sent me a draft of this charter to comment upon. I wrote a comment in which I emphasized that there are no rights without corresponding duties. Therefore, if the Declaration of Human Rights is not to remain an inventory of wishful thinking, as it has often been described, there must be a corresponding declaration of duties and responsibilities for those who have to enforce those rights.

However, for those who were coming out of a period of oppression, the problem was one of asserting rights. Besides, the Universal Declaration of Human Rights was born in such a context, as can be clearly seen from the preamble which contains a strong statement against despotism, 'Whereas disregard and contempt for human rights have resulted in barbarous acts which have outraged the conscience of mankind, . . . '.

V. If you had to write a guide to the duties incumbent upon a citizen, what would be the first duty?

B. The duty to respect others. Overcoming personal self-interest. Accepting others. Tolerance of diversity. The fundamental duty is to realize that we live amongst other people.

V. And what would be the first duty that you would like to teach those who rule over us?

B. A sense of statehood, or in other words, the duty to pursue the common good and not the particular or individual good.

V. The admonishment to those in power that they should pursue the common good is the fundamental principle of republican political thought. It is loudly declared in Lorenzetti's painting in the Sala dei Nove in Siena, which everyone rightly believes to be an excellent distillation of the theory of republican self-government: 'they treat the common good as their lord'.

B. The distinction between good and bad government is based on the principle of the common good. States are good when their rulers aim at the common good, and they are bad when the rulers give priority to their own good or a particular good rather than the common good. The monarch rules over everyone and seeks the good of everyone, while the tyrant considers his own interests or those of his own followers. But all this is a little vague. What actually is this common good? Have you never asked yourself about the nature of the common good? Is it the collective good or is it the good of each citizen?

V. In my book on republicanism,[2] I argued that the common good is neither the good (or interests) of everyone nor a good (or interest) that transcends particular interests, but rather the good of the citizens who wish to live free from personal dependency, and as such it opposes the good of those who wish to domineer. I draw inspiration from Machiavelli, who did not fear social and political conflicts as long as they remained within the boundaries of civilized practice, precisely because he did not consider the common good to be the good of each and every person. He set great store by the verbal conflict that occurred within public bodies. He never developed the idea of an organic community in which individuals worked with a view to the common good, nor did he waste time dreaming up republics where the sovereign decisions were unanimously approved because of the virtue of the citizens.

In other words, the common good is the good of those who wish to live together without dominating or being dominated. It is a rhetorical concept in the sense that it is not a criterion that can be demonstrated incontrovertibly. Besides there are no such concepts in political thought. However, I am very happy for you to exhort those who rule over us to pursue the common good.

The problem is the difficulty in defining moral duty. I believe it useful to distinguish between moral duty and political and juridical obligation. Moral duty is an inner value, in the sense that it is an inner feeling of obligation towards ourselves, towards our consciences. Juridical or political obligation is external in the sense that it is an obligation towards an external authority.

When we say 'I must do this' or 'I must not do that', we mean either that something within ourselves is driving us to do or not to do something, or that there is a power that can force us to do or not do something. The meaning of this distinction is better understood if we consider the nature of the punishment. In the first case – of a duty in the strict sense of the term – it is our conscience (when it exists) that punishes us with remorse. In the second case – of an obligation – it is the sovereign power that punishes us by depriving us of our liberty, our property or even our life.

B.   The distinction you have just mentioned is a classical distinction. Moral duty is a duty of conscience; what is called an inner duty. Juridical duty is an external duty, a duty in relation to another person. If you look at the endless number of books about duty from Cicero onwards, you discover that this distinction recurs time and time again. Samuel Pufendorf in his *Of the Duties of the Man and the Citizen* distinguishes between duties to God, duties of man to himself and the duties of man to his fellow beings. Duties towards God 'are generally limited to the knowledge and worship of this Supreme Being, which means that we need to have the right ideas about His nature and His attributes, and we have to conform with His will in all our actions'.[3] Duties to oneself are founded on the principle that 'in order to celebrate the creator's infinite glory and be a worthy member of human society, man must, in this respect, fulfil some duties in relation to himself...; he must show himself worthy of the noble faculties that distinguish him so advantageously from the animals by carefully cultivating his natural dispositions, and he must, as far as it is possible for him, obtain a condition in which he can contribute to the good of society'.[4] Duties to others are founded on the principle 'of not doing harm to anyone and redressing any harm that might have been caused'.[5] Duty towards others is basically juridical duty, whereas duty to oneself is moral duty in the strict sense. Duty to God is religious duty. It seems to me that this is the fundamental distinction. I have to confess, however, that I do not know why they used *officium* for what we call 'duty'.

When you argued that we talk too much about rights and too little about duties, it occurred to me that in reality there are many more books on duties than on rights when you take into account the Latin word *officium*. Books on rights would have been called *de libertatibus*, because liberties were the Latin equivalent for what we call rights. This is demonstrated by the title of one of the fundamental texts on rights: *Magna Charta de Libertatibus* [Magna Carta].

V.   Neither do I know the reason why they used *officium* for what we call 'duty'. I am struck by the fact that *officium* derives from the verb *officere*, which means 'to impede' or 'to work against'. But against what? Perhaps against oneself, in the sense that fulfilling one's duties involves going against one's natural inclinations. The

Italian term *dovere* derives from *debeo*, which in turn came from *de habere*. This indicates that someone is to have something from us; in other words, it is a debt. In both these terms there is an element of compulsion, and therefore duties are opposed to liberties.

But the point I would like to stress is that, although it is true that many books have been written on duties, it is also the case that Cicero's *De Officiis* was widely read and commented upon in antiquity, whereas modern books on duties such as Mazzini's *Doveri dell'uomo* are considered curiosities. What I mean is that in the Modern Era and more especially in our time, books that deal with duties are not taken very seriously. I am not saying that the ancients had a more profound sense of duty than people have today; it is simply that study into and reflections on duties have little significance and hardly any influence in our times. Perhaps the most important reason for this change in the way we think was suggested by De Sanctis: 'It is a blessed thing to inspire a sense of duty in the people, but at what price? On its own, a sense of duty becomes a sense of servitude. It is a virtue when you unite with another sentiment, a sense of one's own rights. Then, people fulfil their duty because they feel that they have rights.'[6]

B.   There is an historical reason why the study of rights prevailed in political thought. In the history of political thought, the problem of power, or rather the relationship between the rulers and the ruled, was mainly treated from the ruler's point of view (*ex parte principis*). To look at the question of power *ex parte principis* means looking at it from the point of view of the rulers' rights rather than from the citizens' point of view in relation to the rulers. In historical terms, the latter occurred only very recently. You have to wait for the declarations of rights, starting with the Declaration of the Rights of Man and of the Citizen approved by the French Constituent Assembly on 26 August 1789. Only much later did thinkers start to see the power relationship more from the people's point of view (*ex parte populi*) than from the ruler's (*ex parte principis*). Approaching the problem of power *ex parte populi* means from the point of view of the rights of the citizens in relation to the rulers and not from the point of view of the rulers' rights. One of the fundamental themes in political theory in all ages has in fact been that of political obligation: the foundations of, the nature of and the limitations upon political obligation.

V.   Political obligation is not a moral duty.

B.   But it is still a duty. The political obligation is the obligation incumbent upon the subject or citizen in relation to the rulers, an obligation that begs the question of why such an obligation should exist. In modern political thought, the question of duty is far from ignored. I repeat: one of the fundamental questions of political philosophy is that of the political obligation. I recall very well the arguments on the subject put by Alessandro Passerin d'Entrèves, who distinguished between political obligation, juridical obligation and moral obligation.[7] However, leaving aside the distinction between the various types of obligation, the question of obligation is undoubtedly fundamental to modern political philosophy, and therefore the question of duty is far from being ignored.

V.   The duty to serve the common good and engage in acts of solidarity with fellow citizens is a moral duty that cannot be imposed by laws, except indirectly.

B.   Laws impose more negative duties than positive duties: the duty to not do something rather than to do something. Exponents of natural law made a distinction (a mistaken one at that) between law and morality by which morality is composed of positive duties whereas law is composed of negative duties. The criminal code, which we could call the quintessence of the duties of a citizen's duties to the state, is largely made up of negative duties: do not steal, do not kill, and so on.

V. But you have argued that good laws need good morals, because the law alone cannot preserve a good democratic and liberal community. Such a community needs the assistance of that inner sentiment that is a sense of duty. Given that a sense of civil duty is an inner sentiment, how can it be reinforced? It is true that laws do mould moral behaviour by forcing citizens to observe certain rules. It seems to me, however, that a sense of duty needs something other than laws, precisely because of its inner nature. How do we instil a sense of civil duty where it does not exist?

B. Through education, because we start with the assumption that man as an animal needs to be domesticated. Education mainly involves the imposition of duties, and not the encouragement of rights.

V. I believe that civil education requires words, memories and examples. A true educator is simply someone who has moral authority, someone who incurs respect and authoritativeness. Today, where is the moral authority capable of providing teaching based on authoritativeness? Once, parents were the first and most important moral authority, but today it is rare for parents to be able to exercise such authority over their children. Then there was the school: it seems to me that there aren't many teachers today who want or know how to be educators capable of instilling a sense of duty. There were the political parties: with all their defects the old political parties were schools of civil education. Today, the parties only teach their members to obey their leaders. Don't you feel there is a lack of secular moral authorities capable of imparting civil education?

B. There is undoubtedly an absence of moral authority outside the Church. This vacuum is increasingly being filled by religion. The fact that young people are often too cynical, arrogant and consumerist is a product of the emptiness of their lives. When life has no sense, we can become self-destructive.

These are all phenomena that reveal a lack of moral authority. There can be no doubt that the absence of moral authority is in part due to the decline of the old political parties. Consider the past nature of a party such as the Communist Party in terms of an education to the fulfilment of duties. The same can also be said of the Socialist Party, the Christian Democrats and the Republican Party. How can parties such as those of D'Antoni or Mastella gain any moral authority?[8]

But the most serious problem today is that no one is ashamed of anything any more, and we must remember that a sense of shame has always been the demonstration that a moral sense exists.

V.   I remember very well that you often used to hear the expression: 'Aren't you ashamed of yourself?' You never hear that now. That is probably because the reply would be 'But, of course, I am not ashamed. Why should I be ashamed?' The word 'shame' is no longer used.

B.   Indeed. It would be worth reflecting on the concept of shame. Shame is a sentiment that you feel when you have committed an action that your moral conscience condemns.

— 6 —

Fear of God and Love of God

V.   As you have already observed, religion has become
the only reference point within this moral vacuum. Faith
and the certainty arising from dogma have become the
sole moral guide. Even though many Catholics emphasize that faith and doubt go hand in hand, it seems clear
to me that those who have religious faith believe in certain
truths.

   While the distinction between believers and non-
believers is a mistaken one, it is quite right to distinguish
between the secular and the Christian concept of life,
given that secular thought perceives the limits on human
reason as an insurmountable barrier and, above all, it does
not seek assistance in faith to overcome that barrier. Catholics, on the other hand, are not willing to accept such
limits; they demand an answer and they find it in their
faith in Christ. A secularist does not know the truth about
the meaning of life and death, but a Christian does. Christ
said, 'He that believeth on the Son hath everlasting life.'[1]
For Christians, is this a truth or simply an opinion like any
other? If they do not believe in these and other words
of Christ, how can they call themselves Christians? Christians are right when they argue that Catholics and secularists share a sense of the mystery of mankind. The point

is that in relation to this mystery, Catholics accept the assistance of faith, whereas secularists accept that the mystery must remain a mystery.

B.   It is a certainty that is based on the belief that there is only one supreme judge capable of standing in judgement, and He is God. One of the fundamental reasons for carrying out moral actions is what is called fear of God. Take away this fear of God and all people will become libertines. The fear of God is considered an absolutely indispensable element in all societies, because otherwise people will suddenly turn into wild beasts.

V.   There is a particularly disturbing aspect to the reasoning you have just described. It is certainly the case that the exponents of religious morality argue that fear of God is a necessary element in the life of every society. However, it is equally true that in the history of political thought there are important examples of theorists who have argued that the fear of God is particularly necessary in democracies. Machiavelli, to quote the most significant example, criticized Christianity, as interpreted by the Catholic Church, for having preached that the greatest good was to be found 'in humility, abasement, and contempt for the affairs of men' and that strength was the ability 'to suffer more than to carry out an act of force'. This was supposed to have made the 'world weak' and as such easy prey for 'evil men'.[2]

   In spite of this, Machiavelli believed that religion and more especially the fear of God was essential 'for commanding armies, motivating the common people, maintaining the good behaviour of men, and putting the guilty to shame'. He even wrote that divine worship and the fear of God are particularly necessary in republics,

> and just as the observance of divine worship is the cause of
> the greatness of republics, so disdain for it is the cause
> of their ruin. This is because, where there is an absence of

the fear of God, either that state shall collapse or it will have to be held together by fear of a prince who compensates for the deficiencies of the religion.[3]

Three centuries later, Tocqueville praised the clear separation between Church and State, when he was examining the institutions and morals of the United States of America, the first great republic in the modern world. However, he also wrote that what is most important for society is not that all citizens must profess the true religion, but that they profess any religion.[4] He emphasized that America, where religion has an enormous hold over people, is also the 'freest and most enlightened' nation. It is political freedom itself that makes religion necessary: 'For my part, I doubt whether man can ever support at the same time complete religious independence and entire political freedom. And I am inclined to think that if faith be wanting in him, he must be subject; and if he be free, he must believe.'[5] Tocqueville wondered how a society could save itself, 'if the moral tie is not strengthened in proportion as the political tie is relaxed? And what can be done with a people who are their own masters if they are not submissive to the Deity?'[6] Machiavelli and Tocqueville, two writers very far apart, came by a different route to the same conclusion that republics have a particular need of religion to provide the citizens with direction in their moral life and to instil in them a sense of duty that causes the laws to be observed and civil obligations to be fulfilled.

Machiavelli's argument that religion is needed to sustain a sense of duty identifies an important truth: religious belief and fear of God penetrate people's hearts and influence all their actions, whereas political authority and the law using rewards and punishments do not enter their hearts and are restricted to affecting their actions but not their motivations, except perhaps to some limited extent. Unless there is some other force capable of touching inner motives of behaviour, we have to accept the idea that religion is necessary. It seems to me that Machiavelli and

Tocqueville have posed a very grave intellectual and political challenge.

B.   Either the monarch gives his orders from above, and therefore imposes fear or terror, or you have to have religion. Force is the means used by the monarch to impose his will. On this there can be no doubt. Democracy has to substitute fear of the monarch with some other force. Saying that people only observe duties and have a sense of duty inasmuch as they fear the negative consequences of not fulfilling their duties (i.e. punishments that may be imposed by the monarch, criminal law or God) is the same as saying that duties are only enacted out of fear of the consequences of non-fulfilment. Jurists would say that precepts are always in pairs. There is a precept that imposes a duty and there is another that obliges not the individual but the judge – and therefore another person – to provide a sentence.

Jurists talk of primary precepts and secondary precepts. The primary precept says, 'do not kill'; the secondary precept says, 'anyone who has killed must be subjected to a specific punishment'. The primary precept is made complete as a duty by the secondary norm that refers to the judge. In the case of a moral duty, the secondary precept refers to God, in that God will impose the punishment and God's punishment will be in the next world.

For the superstitious, however, the punishment might even be in this world. It is common to claim that disease and natural calamity are God's retribution. The retribution of God is perceived by the superstitious as punishment for a duty that has not been fulfilled. Duty is always linked to the possible unpleasant or dishonourable consequences of non-fulfilment.

The law is founded on the twin principle I have just explained. Indeed, the Criminal Code is not made up of primary precepts at all, but rather secondary ones. The Criminal Code does not say that you must not kill. It says that those who kill shall be punished in a certain manner.

V. The conclusion of what you have just said is that the fear that must hold a republic or democracy together (let's take the two concepts as synonyms) is fear of the law, which is something different from fear of the monarch. The monarch is a visible authority who does not derive his legitimacy from the consent of the citizens and is not equal to the others. The law is impersonal and is made by citizens who are like the others. This means that it is difficult for democratic republics to impose the rule of law, which in my opinion is the primary and most important duty of those who govern and hold public office.

The ideal of the rule of law is another promise that democracy has not maintained, to use one of your own expressions. In all contemporary democracies to a greater or lesser extent (and certainly to a lesser extent in our own), there has been a worrying inability to apply the principle of the rule of law in the most elementary sense of the expression: that everyone, both the powerful and the ordinary citizens, are subject to the law and crimes are punished in accordance with the laws. I believe that Beccaria's ideas are still valid:

> One of the greatest restraints on crimes is not the cruelty of punishments, but the inevitability that they will be applied and consequently the vigilance of magistrates. In order to be a useful virtue, that severity of an unfailing judge must be accompanied by mild legislation. The certainty of a punishment, even a mild one, will always make a greater impression than fear of a more terrible punishment, when there is hope of impunity. The reason is that even small harms frighten the human spirit, when they are inevitable, whereas hope, a heavenly gift that often takes complete hold of us, always diminishes the idea of greater harms, when it is encouraged by impunity, often in collusion with avarice and frailty.

He added some interesting considerations on forgiveness:

Some [judges] do not punish small crimes, when the injured parties have pardoned them. This accords with human charity, but is contrary to the public good, for it almost suggests that a private citizen can not only forego compensation for the injury, but also remove, by his pardon, the need for a public example. The right to punish does not belong to a single person, but to all the citizens, or to the sovereign. The private citizen can only renounce his portion of the law, and cannot annul that of others . . . . [Clemency] . . . is a power of the legislator and not those who implement the law. It must dignify the law, and not specific judgements. To show men that crimes can be pardoned or that punishment will not necessarily be the outcome is to encourage the insidious hope of impunity; it will lead people to believe that, because crimes can be forgiven, it is an abuse of power and not an act of justice when they are not.[7]

As Beccaria's words so clearly suggest, the most serious result of the erosion of the rule of law is the spread of a sense of insecurity.

B.   There is an increasing fear that crimes are not punished. There can be no doubt that security is one of citizenry's fundamental needs. Security means that criminals are punished, and the appropriate sanctions applied to those who do not fulfil their duties. This does not always occur in Italy. You only need to think of all the corruption that on the whole goes unpunished.

In any society, and therefore also a democratic society, the fundamental function of the law is to establish the rules for the use of force. The rules on the use of force are: *who* must exercise the use of force (not anyone, but only those authorized to exercise it); *how* (with an orderly judgement); *when* (not at any time, but when the procedures proscribed by the law have been completed); *to what extent* (you cannot punish a petty theft in the same way that you would punish a murder).

In a constitutional state, one of the most important functions of the law is to establish how the state's monopoly of legitimate force is to be used. In a despotic society, there is no such rule; a monarch can punish without checks and without limits. His power is arbitrary.

V.   Montesquieu identifies the sovereign's power to punish and reward without restriction as a distinctive feature of despotism. Montesquieu defines the laws in a despotic state as 'the sovereign's capricious and fleeting will'.[8]

B.   In a constitutional state, the law must regulate the use of force available to the state, so that it does not become an arbitrary force.

V.   The problem is that if a democratic state is not capable of punishing violations of the law in accordance with the principles that you have listed, then the majority wishes to see not crimes punished in accordance with justice, but exemplary punishments, unlimited punishments and the maximum penalty, which is the death penalty. In my opinion, it is essential that a democratic society is capable of punishing in accordance with justice in order to avoid increasing demand for justice to be enacted by individuals, or entrusted to private agencies or some 'saviour of society'.

B.   Which would mean a return to the state of nature, to the war of everyone against everyone ('bellum omnium contra omnes').

V.   As your Hobbes wrote.

B.   In the Hobbesian state of nature, everyone can punish everyone else on the basis of natural law. Hobbes defined natural law (*ius naturale*) as 'the Liberty each man hath, to use his own power, as he will himselfe, for the preservation of his own Nature; that is to say, of his own Life; and consequently of doing any thing, which in his own

Judgement, and Reason, hee shall conceive to be the aptest means thereunto'.[9]

V.   This is precisely the reason why I cannot understand the considerable reluctance in Italy to grasp the need to punish in accordance with the law. Perhaps it is because I live in the United States, a country that often inflicts excessive punishments, particularly in the case of the death sentence, but I feel that in Italy there is diffidence towards the very principle of legality. I recall a memorable passage from Tocqueville:

> in the United States everyone is personally interested in enforcing the obedience of the whole community to the law; for as the minority may shortly rally the majority to its principles, it is interested in professing that respect for the decrees of the legislator which it may soon have occasion to claim for its own. However irksome an enactment may be, the citizen of the United States complies with it, not only because it is the work of the majority, but because it is his own, and he regards it as a contract to which he himself is party.[10]

In contrast, those who punish in accordance with the law – the inflexible judge and the scrupulously honest politicians – are not figures that evoke sincere admiration in the Italian mind. The hero is more likely to be someone who cunningly gets round the law or uses his power to put himself above it.

B.   Indeed, comic characters who play the part of the typical Italian are people who escape the law and manage to get away with things. Do you remember that famous film, *Il sorpasso*?[11] Law-breaking is considered a demonstration of virility and therefore behaviour to be applauded. I don't want to take the discussion back to fascism, but I believe that the recent origins of this mentality that praises law-breaking are to be found in fascism.

V.   I agree. Wasn't the breaking of boundaries one of the typical features of fascism? Besides, their motto was 'I couldn't give a toss'.

B.   We even had a party founded on this motto, a party that eventually took power. I believe this to be a unique example in the world.

V.   This brings to mind that in English there is an expression in current use that has the opposite meaning. It is 'I care', and it has recently been taken up by Veltroni.[12] I could write an appendix to your book, *Left and Right,*[13] that demonstrates how the contrast between fascism and antifascism is mirrored very closely by the contrast between 'I couldn't give a toss' and 'I care'.

The fascist mentality is the opposite of the one that values the idea of caring for one's community and fellow citizens. On this point of caring, I recently wrote an article in which I ask whether we secularists haven't perhaps opened the door to this massive return to religious devotion by not giving convincing answers to the question of what we now call solidarity.

Catholics talk of solidarity, charity and compassion, and what is more they put these into practice. What do we secularists do? Do we have a concept of charity, compassion and solidarity that differs from the Catholic one? I believe there is an important difference between Christian charity and secular charity. Christian charity is Christ who shares your suffering. Secular charity is also the sharing of suffering, but in addition it is indignation directed against those who are responsible for such suffering.

This indignation provides an inner force to fight against the causes of suffering. Precisely because persons without religious faith do not see any value in human suffering caused by other human beings and do not believe in the possibility or value of a reward in another life, secular charity not only seeks to lessen the suffering of the oppressed, but also to remedy that suffering, if that is at all possible. It encourages the oppressed to struggle against the causes of oppression.

B.   It seems to me that you are contrasting charity with justice. This is an important subject for secular thought. Charity leaves things as they are; it lessens the suffering, but does not take any action to root out the causes. It provides assistance where there is suffering. You talk of charity when illustrating the need to fight the causes of suffering, but it would be more correct to speak of a sense of justice that expresses the need to use the law to change the way things are.

When charity was dominant, church steps were full of the crippled, the lame and the blind. There are plenty of pictorial images to demonstrate this. However, I would never deny that charitable works have had an important role, and still do to this day. Take the Cottolengo Homes, for instance.[14] There is no secular association that has founded a comparable institution.

V.   Without doubt, Catholics can now proclaim: 'We practise solidarity, while you secularists theorize justice. Indeed, you secularists assert that for reasons imposed by the market it is increasingly difficult for states to guarantee social rights.' If we accept this argument, we have to conclude that the most convincing solution is the one provided by the Catholics. No problem there, but is it really the best solution? I am not entirely convinced that the secular response to Catholic charity is justice rather than a different concept of charity. I continue to believe that there is a secular interpretation of charity that differs from the Catholic one, in that it does not only aim to share and alleviate suffering, but also aims to foster a sense of indignation and to give strength to the oppressed, so that they can fight against the causes of oppression. The meaning of charity in its highest sense must impart the will to resist oppression and must above all encourage the oppressed to resist. On the other hand, you advise me not to contrast

Christian charity with a secular concept of charity, but to invoke the ideal of justice.

B.   Christianity, interpreted in its highest sense which is that of the Gospel, is more powerful than secularism. As a secularist, you assert your non-belief and proclaim that religion is superstition. 'Well,' the believer will respond, 'as far as this life is concerned, why don't you go into one of the many existing institutions to do good works in a completely disinterested manner?' Many religious people do good works unselfishly, although they are inspired by the idea that such good works will bring them God's blessing. We cannot promise God's blessing. We cannot promise anything to those who carry out good works unselfishly, except the satisfaction of having fulfilled a duty and the pleasure of the good works themselves. When secularists put their arguments to me, I always ask: 'But would you be able to do what believers do out of an inspiration that is not concerned with their personal interests, perhaps in the hope of some reward in the next world?' It may be that the hope of some divine favour we cannot provide is decisive.

V.   If, however, we look at the history of the socialist and republican movements, we realize that in the past, in a past that isn't even that distant, there were many people who devoted their lives to teaching the illiterate to read and write, organizing trade unions and establishing co-operative stores. These people were called 'apostles', and they were not seeking to train revolutionary activists. They wanted to mitigate what they called social evils and, at the same time, they wanted to instil in the poor and underprivileged the awareness of a human dignity to be acquired and asserted through organization, commitment, struggle and dialogue with the political adversary. True enough, this aspect of the secular political mission has disappeared in the last few decades.

B.   The phenomenon you refer to concerns part of the nineteenth and twentieth centuries. This is very little compared with the charity that has been provided in the name of Christ. Secularists cannot claim the same merits as Catholics when it comes to charitable works. The reason for this weakness of secularism also depends on the fact that, as I was just saying, secularists have nothing to offer other than the satisfaction of one's conscience. The continuing existence of the practice of indulgences, which we consider scandalous, is proof that people still believe in a reward in the next world. Is it a deception? It is for us, but people believe in it all the same.

V. But don't you think it better to have social rights guaranteed by laws rather than entrusting the care of the sick, the old, the weak and children to some form of joint responsibility – to the charitable inclinations of individuals and associations? From a republican point of view, social rights should not be confused with welfare, which creates lifelong protégés of the state, permits privileges and does not encourage individuals to look after themselves. Nor should they be confused with public charity (and still less with private charity), which provides help as an act of goodwill on the part of the state. Public (and private) charity, however praiseworthy, is incompatible with civilized existence, because it offends against the dignity of the recipient. If I need assistance because I am poor, ill, old or alone, I would prefer that assistance to be the acknowledgement of my right as a citizen, rather than based on a decision of an individual in the name of Christ's love. It is not an offence to be ill or old, and although many people do not understand this, a republic is not a public limited company, but a form of communal living whose aim is the dignity of its citizens. This is why a republic has the duty to guarantee assistance, not as an act of compassion, but as the acknowledgement of a right that derives from being a citizen. It therefore has to take on the burden of assisting its citizens, without making the recipients feel they are a burden and without handing over to private agencies duties for which it should be responsible. Mazzini's comment on public and private charity is still valid:

> Christian charity was more a means to improve one's soul than an awareness of a common aim to be achieved, with God's will, on this earth. It never went beyond charity. When misfortunes befell men of the new religion, it fed the hungry, it clothed the ragged and it cared for the sick, but it did not think about how to remove the reasons for poverty and lack of clothing.[15]

Don't you think it preferable to receive assistance in the name of rights rather than out of charity?

B. It may be preferable, but reality is different. The reality is that female voluntary home visitors ['le dame di San Vincenzo'] go out to some sick old person in a small rented accommodation. What you're talking about is utopia.

V. Not always. There are forms of home care for the sick and the elderly that are organized and funded by local government. They are social workers who bring medicine and food. They stop and chat, and provide a bit of company. They may not be perfect, but I know from personal experience that they do a lot of good, mainly because they make it possible for the old or sick person to stay at home.

B. It seems to me that home care is completely inadequate in relation to demand. Yet real help has to be taken to the home, and certainly does not mean taking the old person to a hospital or a rest home. I have become a friend and patron of a secular association (called Abitare Insieme, or 'Living Together'), which is involved with helping old people in the home and organizes the University of the Third Age. I believe and have written that help in the home is essential. I think about my own condition as an old person, and I realize how much pleasure I get out of staying at home and being helped in the home – in the house where I have always lived and which I can move around with my eyes shut. My home is where I have lived my life. It would be terrible if they uprooted me.

V. What you have just said leads me to re-emphasize my previous arguments that social rights are not compatible with charitable practices. My defence of the principle of social rights (not its implementation in practice, which has lent itself to many well-founded criticisms) was directed against those who argue that private charity and charity provided by associations of civil society could replace social rights. I believe that there is a need for social rights upheld by the laws of the Republic and financed from the public purse, and there is also need for charity provided by voluntary associations. If we intend to entrust welfare entirely to voluntary associations, we will return to the reality you have already described: the Church steps crowded with the needy and the destitute, faith schools and hospitals staffed predominately or entirely with nuns.

B. My father was a doctor, and he always had to deal with nuns. Occasionally they were imperious, but it is also true that they were motivated by a profound Christian vocation: I repeat, they were inspired by Christ and not Mazzini.

V. I persist with the idea that service, *officium*, and care, *cultus*, came before Christianity. To be precise, these were principles in Roman public ethics.[16] This is why I continue to argue that there is a secular concept of charity. You will reply that the secular ideal has remained a mere ideal, whereas Christian charity has been a reality for centuries.

B. It is a reality that has persisted for centuries precisely because it is religious. You can have all the secular beliefs you like, but the strength that derives from religious inspiration and the conviction of being in the service of Christ is much more intense and lasting. People who go and help charitable institutions are generally religious people acting out of love of God and not fear of God. Love of God is a powerful force. Then there are the missionaries. What drives missionaries to go to the most dangerous parts of Africa to set up schools and hospitals? Many of them sacrificed their lives. I remember a colleague of mine, who was a priest and taught the History of Christianity. There came a stage in his life when he felt the need to be something more than a university lecturer and he resigned from the university. He then went to be a missionary in one of the poorest countries in the world.

V.   I only know of one other ideology that was able to evoke a spirit of dedication and sacrifice in men and women that was comparable with the one that religious faith is still capable of evoking, and that was communism. Consider the great number of people who abandoned or sacrificed family and profession to become activists. Do you see any parallels?

B.   Certainly, communism has often been described as a new religion. Besides, the Gospels say that those who wish to follow Jesus must abandon their parents.[17]

V.   I am the first to applaud those who do charitable works in the name of religion, as long as they don't say, 'we're the only people who are needed' or 'give us the public resources and you'll see that we will use them far more wisely than the republic'. Besides, social rights did not come as a gift. They had to be fought for with the sacrifices of men and women, believers and non-believers who wanted to live their lives on this earth in dignity.

B.   But the fact remains that religious inspiration is a tremendous force.

V.   In your article on religion in *Micromega*,[18] you drew attention to the fact that a secularist who accepts that human experience is finite takes on a highly moral concept of life precisely because he or she accepts the finite nature of life. You describe the sense of mystery as a fundamental aspect of the secularist's religiosity, while that sense of mystery is to some extent destroyed by faith, because faith provides an answer. Isn't it better to leave intact that sense of mystery which turns into melancholy?

B.   The clergy itself places great importance on mystery and doubt. Cardinal Martini often talks of faith and doubt. I am not at all convinced by his distinction between believers and non-believers. What does non-believer mean? It means someone who believes in something different from what you believe. The real, insurmountable distinction is between Christians and secularists. It is a profound distinction. Secularists do not have faith.

V.   And yet the distinction between believers and non-believers returned in a debate between Pietro Scoppola and Alberto Asor Rosa.[19] Pietro Scoppola argued that:

> Believers and non-believers share a sense of the mystery of mankind, something that is beyond our powers of knowledge and our possible actions. Here we find our common human matter, this open humanism, which seems to me to be the primary condition....I do not believe that believers and non-believers are divided by a Berlin Wall. The believer does not hold the truth in his pocket, and for his part, the non-believer cannot help being aware of those nagging doubts over how to approach the great questions concerning the meaning of life. Where is the barrier? We are all on the same side.

Alberto Asor Rosa, with whom he was having the debate, responded that the division between secularists and

Catholics 'is to be found in certain events in our history, when the distinction between the two positions had a real foundation'. He added:

> I believe however that today this distinction and the two categories that justified it are substantially a thing of the past.... There continues to be a distinction between believers and non-believers and between those with faith and those without, but that distinction no longer corresponds to the distinction between secularists and Catholics – at least not in the strict meaning of those terms.

In my opinion, the distinction between believers and non-believers is misleading. Someone who does not believe in the word of God, believes in other words. For example, those who believe in liberty, but not in Christ, believe in the same manner as those who believe in Christ. If words have meaning, as I believe they do, to speak of believers and non-believers is in practice to accept the Christian prejudice that anyone who does not have religious faith cannot hold either solid moral principles or sincere belief, that such a person is simply a '*non*-believer'.

B.   When I think of something that transcends me, I think of humanity. I reflect on the history of mankind, which is a history I am part of. This history has something tragic about it that I try to understand, in spite of its complexity. For me everything is so human that I even believe that religion itself is a product of humanity. Faith in humanity is everything. We are human beings amongst human beings. That is where we have to look for good and evil. I am pessimistic about the question of evil. The struggle for life, which also affects human history, is based on violence. Can original sin provide an explanation? Where is God? I would like Catholics to pose this question. Why is there so much suffering? Does Providence exist? Really? Do the Catholics and the Pope ask themselves these questions? I believe that someone who has faith is also unable to reply to these questions. Those who have faith maintain their faith even when faced with evidence to the contrary. This is why I do not trust those who have faith. Faith blinds people. It is such a powerful light that it blinds them. Once you have been dazzled by the bright light, you cannot discern anything any more. When, on the other hand, you put your faith to one side and start to use reason, you become aware of the uncontainable evil of this world. There are the famous pages of Schopenhauer on evil nature. Evil exists; it is there, and you cannot deny it.

You can easily explain it with the existence of God, but an omnipotent God who is beyond good and evil. But how can a God, such as the Christian God who is merciful and fatherly, allow all this to happen? I can understand an omnipotent God. I can understand calling God the enormous mystery of the universe of which science knows so little. The greater our knowledge becomes, the greater the awareness of our ignorance. We know nothing. We only know that there is this great power. Consider the star-covered sky, the famous image used by Kant. But stars are not what we see. There are thousands upon thousands of galaxies, millions upon millions of heavenly bodies at distances measured in light years. When faced with all this, you know that you know nothing, and therefore you tell yourself that something is eluding you. But this is beyond good and evil. Good and evil are categories invented by human beings in order to live together. Can you imagine the Ten Commandments in relation to the immensity of space? You cannot analyse the immensity of space from the point of view of good and evil. It would be completely senseless. A star collapses and dies. A meteorite falls on another world and destroys all life. How can you judge all this from the point of view of good and evil? You would have your work cut out, if you tried to show that there is order in the universe. Why are there all these abnormalities and solar catastrophes? How are you going to judge them in terms of good and evil? Everything that occurs in the enormous space of the universe is elusive and cannot be classified according to our system of good and evil.

V.   There is no need of absolute moral truths founded on some revelation to give meaning to life and to commitment. The truths are the ones that each of us feel to be moral truths. A profound conviction, although not absolute, can make someone act with strength and consistency comparable to those of someone who lives by religious inspiration. If you really believe in an ideal, the ideal of liberty for instance, you do not need anything else in order to act in the defence of liberty.

B.   This is true. There are many examples of people who have died for liberty.

V.   And they were not believers in the religious meaning of the term.

B.   The secular concept of life has great dignity, but it does not drive people to charitable works. I do not do charitable works. I might talk about them, but I don't actually get round to doing them. There are many priests who do good works such as visiting the sick for their entire lives. Why do they do it, while I don't? Perhaps it is because I am not religious, or rather that I am religious in that I have a sense of the mystery that surrounds us, but my religiosity goes no further than that.

V.   You say that it is one thing to talk, and quite another to act, but Christianity began with the word and arose out of teaching.

B.   However, action, self-sacrifice, sacrifice of one's life, the abandonment of all one's worldly interests to devote oneself entirely to the suffering and the sick, are all things that I encounter in people who have religious convictions. There is a limit. It is one thing to be good, even charitable, and quite another to devote one's entire life to other people. I feel that in a way I lack something by not being religious, because I can see that religious people undoubtedly have something more than I have. Is it perhaps a question of selfishness? Selfishness in the sense that my actions in favour of others are very circumscribed and limited to my family and my wife. They certainly do not stretch as far as any other person. I acknowledge this limitation, and yet I resist the idea of faith. My perception of life is profane and not sacred.

V.   What do you mean by an awareness of the sacred?

B.   Awareness of the sacred means that there are two parallel histories. There is the history that we experience and study in history books, and there is another hidden history that exists in spite of being hidden.

V.   Where is this hidden history written?

B.   I have no idea, but religious people know where it is written. For those who have faith, go to church, believe in miracles and obey the Pope, there is a sacred history alongside profane history. To believe in this history means to have an awareness of the sacred. The sacred goes beyond this world. The difference between the sacred and the profane should be examined in depth and under-stood, because many people believe in a sacred history, although for me it is another mystery of faith.

V.   It is an illusion founded on hope and is evoked by words – by the words of those who believe. During funeral rites, a priest pronounces words that touch the family and friends of the departed very deeply. He says that they will meet up again with their dear one in another life and there will be the resurrection of the body. You see how the belief in sacred history is generated by words that have an enor-mous persuasive power. What other words would you want to hear in such a moment, other than that your dear departed has not gone away forever and you will meet again? Those words are extremely powerful. No secular person could say anything of equal force and ability to create hope at a time of the deepest desperation, when the misery of the death of someone we love makes us realize the harsh and sorrowful nature of profane history. When faced with death, we have a particular need of hope, and ministers of the faith know the very words that can give us hope in another history, which is, of course, this sacred history.

B.   There is a dimension to life, which I call sacred as opposed to profane, that the secularist does not experience. I really have had no experience of it. As far as I am concerned, death is death.

V.   You have written that if we accept the idea of resurrection, then death is no longer death.[20]

B.   The idea that the soul survives the body is a classical one. We find it in Plato's *Phaedo*. A man's body is the soul's tomb. The idea that the soul is free once the body has been destroyed is a very old one. It is possible to attempt an explanation of this myth. Plato could not possibly have known that ideas were formed in his brain. For him they were a reality that came from he knew not where, but certainly not from his body.

The last century was dominated by the idea that religion was the opiate of the people. Is there still anyone who has the courage to argue this view? It may not be the opiate of the people, but it is perhaps something worse: the drug of the people. An opiate puts you to sleep, but drugs can kill. Look at what is happening in the conflict between Palestinians and Jews, as a result of religious extremists on both sides. When you get close to a solution, the extremists kill. Religion often leads to crime. The young man who killed Rabin said, 'God ordered me to do it.' This is sufficient to demonstrate that religion is not the opiate of the people, but very possibly something worse.

V. Religion has been and still is the cause of immense suffering.

B. The Pope has asked for forgiveness for the Church's mistakes on several occasions, but if there is guilt, then it is indelible. It is there, and it stays there. The idea that sins are stains on the soul that confession washes away, as they used to tell me when I was a boy, is an idea that reduces sin to a trifle.

V. There can be no doubt of that. Besides, I don't think that either of us has an optimistic concept of history. I believe more in a cyclical concept, similar to the tides. For a while things get better, but then they slip backwards again. Progress and decadence alternate. When I talk of decadence, I think of moral and civil decadence, but above all I think of the unleashing of violence and war, which I consider to be the worst evil of them all.

B. Hegel believed that history was the history of freedom, but he also had a realistic sense of history and wrote in the introduction to his *Philosophy of History*: 'History has always been an immense slaughterhouse.'

— 7 —

The Republic and its Problems

V. Any dialogue on the republic worthy of the name must confront the problems that afflict our civic life and, if possible, suggest some remedies. Following the example of classical authors, it appears to me that the most serious threat to the survival of a democratic republic comes from factionalism, where factions are understood to be groups of men loyal to a single leader, whose principal aim is to obtain advantage and privilege. The danger posed by factions lies in this pursuit of advantage and privilege, and in their members' loyalty to the leader. I think that we are now witnessing a return of factions in the form of 'personal parties', as you have defined them. By far the clearest example of this is the political organization called Forza Italia.[1]

Francesco Guicciardini, who knew more than a little about politics, wrote:

> While only men's faces and outer colours change, the same things all recur again and again, and we never see any event that has not occurred in some other time. But this changing of names and the outer shape of things means that only the prudent recognize their return. This is why history is valuable and useful, because it confronts you with what you have not known or seen, and it makes it possible for you to recognize such events.[2]

Let's be prudent and try to understand: what previously seen political phenomenon is hidden under the new name and new colours of personal parties and Forza Italia?

B.   When I speak of a 'personal party', I mean to emphasize that it is a party created by a single person in contrast to a party in the real sense of the term, which is by definition an association of persons. A personal party has nothing to do with the fact that parties have a leader or more than one leader. All parties have a leader, as has been explained by Robert Michels.[3] Indeed, a party with more than one leader is considered abnormal. Christian Democracy, which was the great party that dominated Italian political life for years, always had several leaders. For this reason, it was seen as unusual, while the standard party has a single leader. You only have to think of Nenni in the Italian Socialist Party, Togliatti and later Berlinguer in the Italian Communist Party, and Ugo La Malfa in the Republican Party. A party cannot exist without a leader. But Forza Italia and D'Antoni's party, which is the most recent example, are something very different from the old parties with their leaders.

V.   The parties you just mentioned had leaders, but they did not live for their leaders and by virtue of their leaders. In fact, throughout their histories they had several leaders. In the case of personal parties, the party lives for the leader and by virtue of the founding leader. It is always risky to venture into predictions, but I believe that in the case of these parties, if the founding leader disappears, then the party will also disappear. If Berlusconi leaves the political stage, I think that Forza Italia would melt away like snow on a sunny day or at least split up into several different parties. The disappearance of a leader did not challenge the very existence of traditional parties. This difference can be explained by the fact that the old parties not only had leaders, but also ideologies, collective memories and solid organizational structures.

B.   Berlusconi's is a personal party in the strict sense of the term, in that it is not an association that has created a leader, but a leader who has created an association.

V.   Because of this, the nature of the loyalty that binds activists and party members to the party leader is very different.

B.   Berlusconi knows very well that a personal party cannot survive for very long. This is why he is transforming the party and attempting to get it to put down roots around the country. Whereas the old mass parties have ceased to be mass parties, the personal party might become a mass party in the traditional sense of the term.

V.   Forza Italia, not to mention the other personal parties, lacks an ideology, at least for the moment, and it needs one to bring it closer into line with the traditional parties. By ideology I mean a set of shared principles, some perception of the future and the past.

B.   I believe that Forza Italia has an ideology. It may only be a negative ideology of anti-statism as opposed to the statism that Berlusconi attributes entirely to the left, but nevertheless an ideology. An anti-statist ideology in the name of the free market is persuasive, even if based on a negative approach, partly because Berlusconi has identified statism with communism and has managed to convince people that Italy, having been statist, was also communist. This means that freeing Italy from communism also requires freeing it from statism.

V.   The old parties had a pantheon of illustrious political figures of the past; they had a past. They could appeal to a tradition, particularly in difficult moments, in order to restore lost values, to renew themselves in the name of their founding principles or to legitimize decisions to re-launch themselves. Today, there are practically no important parties that can appeal to such a pantheon, least of all Berlusconi's. Do you believe that he will attempt to build his own theoretical and political tradition, perhaps by borrowing figures from other parties?

B.   Forza Italia is a reaction to the existing state of affairs. Fascism was also an avowedly new movement, one that arose from a reaction to the social and political reality during the years immediately following the First World War. Berlusconi's party was founded to wind up the First Republic. One of the reasons for Berlusconi's strength (and in my opinion also the danger he presents) is that he marked a new stage in the country's history. He was the founder of a new party in contrast with the old parties, which were considered decadent, and he presented himself as such, just as the Fascists presented themselves in relation to the old parties of liberal Italy.

V.   Mussolini actually proclaimed himself the enemy of decadent democracy.

B.   Mussolini considered the other parties to be finished, to have fulfilled their task. He announced the need for a generalized renewal. The birth of Forza Italia is in this sense very similar to the birth of the Fascist Party, in the sense of being a new party, as I have explained. Even though it defines itself as the party of freedom, and indeed the central pillar of the Polo delle Libertà,[4] Forza Italia in no way refers back to the Italian tradition of liberalism. It has nothing in common with the liberalism of Einaudi, just to refer to one of the most important names.[5] Nor does it have the features of a traditional conservative party. Forza Italia is therefore a subversive party, and Berlusconi is well aware of this.

V.   In my opinion, the subversive nature of Forza Italia arises from the fact that it is a party founded on unconditional loyalty to its leader, and not to an idea, project or utopia that transcends the leader. It is my impression that Forza Italia's local politicians, canvassers and supporters feel loyal to Silvio Berlusconi and not to an idea. The party managers and activists in the old communist, socialist and republican parties were primarily committed to upholding ideas and interests, and not to supporting Berlinguer, Nenni or La Malfa.[6]

Obviously there was also loyalty based on political patronage in the parties of the First Republic, particularly in the case of the Christian Democrats. In the political jargon of the time, people were referred to as followers of Fanfani, Forlani, De Mita and Andreotti [*fanfaniani, forlaniani, demitiani, andreottiani*, etc.]. Apart from the fact that there were several leaders rather than one, the patronage (in the traditional sense of a patron who hands out favours to his *clientes* who pay court and offer the loyalty) and the personalized nature of the Christian Democrats (and other parties too, to a greater or lesser extent) were considered to be an example of corruption in Italian political life. Today, in contrast, public opinion accepts the existence of a large personal party founded on loyalty to *a single* leader, without the slightest sign of astonishment. A political phenomenon that anyone with a modicum of civic conscience should find highly disturbing is accepted as perfectly normal.

B.   Berlusconi not only founded a personal party, but also does everything he can to emphasize this personal nature of Forza Italia. This is demonstrated by the fact that his face is displayed everywhere, a face that is always smiling and always self-assured. His has been blessed by God, or rather, as he has himself proclaimed, 'anointed by the Lord'.

V.   There is another feature of Berlusconi's party that has considerable parallels with the totalitarian movements. I am referring to the fact that the word of Silvio Berlusconi is believed as though it had a prophetic quality. He can announce the most ridiculous lies and still be believed. He has always claimed that from 1945 until he became Prime Minister, Italy was governed by communists, and there are millions of Italians who believe him and trust him.

B. A personality cult is typical of a charismatic leader. Mussolini was undoubtedly a charismatic leader. When he appeared on the balcony, he gained the applause of the crowd and entered into a dialogue with them. He gave short, extremely incisive speeches, and he asked questions of the crowd, to which they had to answer either yes or no, according to the expectations. Mussolini knew what the crowd's response would be. He knew how to communicate with the crowd, something that was much less true of Hitler who was much more distant from the crowd. He was a celestial power. Stalin, too, did not have a direct rapport with his people. We always saw him attending a military parade or on the great balcony of the Palace of State, almost unfailingly in military uniform along with his leading officials. Stalin never entered into a dialogue with his people. You never saw him in front of applauding Russian communists. He always had the same glacial expression. He was truly the leader that came down from above. I always saw him as taciturn, and in this sense he was very different from Mussolini and Hitler. Leaders of the Bolshevik Party were great orators, with the exception of Stalin who did not go in for speeches.

V. The historic leaders of the October Revolution were a product of European socialism, which was, amongst other things, a great school of eloquence. Socialist leaders and activists had to be orators capable of explaining the party's political strategy, but above all they had to be capable of engendering enthusiasm, hope and indignation, which are typically revolutionary emotions. Mussolini himself was trained in the socialist tradition. It was when he was a socialist that he learnt the art of exciting the crowd.

When he became a fascist, he used the same art to evoke nationalistic passions rather than revolutionary ones.

B.   A revolution requires a great demagogue. Max Weber distinguished between three types of charismatic leader: the religious prophet, the great demagogue and the military leader.[7] Mussolini was primarily a great demagogue. Stalin was primarily a military leader, or at least he liked to think of himself as one. He always appeared in uniform, and liked to show off his medals. As for the religious prophet, Mao was perhaps partly one.

V.   Some great democratic leaders had the characteristics of religious prophets. Think of Mazzini, who founded his entire theory of duties and social emancipation on the concept of God. Think of Martin Luther King, to give a more recent example. Martin Luther King developed a Christian form of expression as a powerful contribution to the struggle of American blacks for emancipation. He used biblical texts to strengthen his supporters and make them capable of overcoming the many obstacles they encountered in their struggle for emancipation. In one of his texts, he preached that American blacks had to be 'as innocent as doves and as cunning as snakes' and that they had to avoid weakness because weak individuals believe that the only way to deal with oppression is to adapt to it. They are acquiescent and resigned in the face of segregation. They prefer to remain oppressed. Luther King used to say to his followers that when Moses led the Children of Israel out of slavery in Egypt to the Promised Land, he realized that slaves do not always love their liberators. They prefer to put up with the evils they know, rather than confront new ones. They prefer the 'flesh pots of Egypt' to the hard work of emancipation. He continuously stresses that passive acceptance of an unjust system means supporting that system and therefore becoming part of the evil. It is indeed a religious discourse very different from the one that Machiavelli so strongly disapproved of because it made people submissive.

— 72 —

Like the founders of states and the legendary legislators Machiavelli admired, Martin Luther King considered God to be on his side and on the side of the oppressed who he wanted to lead to emancipation. When King and other leaders of the movement were on trial in Montgomery (Alabama) for having organized the famous boycott of buses, news that the Supreme Court had ruled that racial segregation on buses was unconstitutional arrived just before the court was about to pronounce its sentence. King greeted this sensational news with the words: 'God Almighty has spoken from Washington.' The Supreme Court ruling became, through King's words, a sign that God was on the side of the civil-rights movement.[8]

B.   Martin Luther King was a democratic religious leader, even though his battle was not primarily political, unless we use the word in its widest possible sense. His battle was to attain freedom from racial segregation; it was a battle for emancipation. King was a prophet who marched at the head of his people, and was then killed, like the great religious leader Gandhi. A political leader can easily die in his bed, like Stalin.

V.   Going back to our charismatic leader, we can conclude that he has the characteristics of a classical demagogue rather than those of a religious prophet, in spite of his claim to have been 'anointed by the Lord'. To be acknowledged a religious prophet and to convince people that you have been inspired by God, you require impeccable behaviour and a saintly life, as with Savonarola.[9] I believe – I very much hope – that Berlusconi will not succeed in persuading people that he is gifted with a prophetic spirit, and I base that hope on the simple fact that he lacks a saintly life. It seems to me that we are faced with another example of an oligarchic demagogue.[10]

B.   If we use Weber's classification, Berlusconi comes under the category of demagogue.

V.   He brings to mind another great popular, rather than oligarchic, demagogue, who proclaimed himself to be 'the man of providence', the man of extraordinary qualities, who has come to free an oppressed people.

B.   A people that has fallen into the hands of the communists.

V.   Berlusconi inspires enthusiasm; he is not simply someone who gathers votes.

B.   There can be no doubt that he inspires enthusiasm. This can be seen when he appears before his followers, particularly when on stage. The ceremony, the hand movements and the smile are those of a charismatic leader. He can laugh even at the jokes that are directed against him. He has boundless self-confidence. He is capable of extracting himself from any embarrassing situation.

V.   The ability to make the people laugh and to laugh with them is typical once again of the demagogue and the flatterer.

B.   Stalin certainly had no sense of humour. Mussolini had vulgar wit; he mocked his opponents and emphasized their weaknesses, particularly physical ones. He loved to spark coarse laughter. Fascists, in general, loved obscene language. However, it does not appear that Mussolini was good at telling jokes; it was rather that he was sarcastic when dealing with his enemies.

V.   Democracies are particularly susceptible to or prone to create the vulgar politician. The very quality of the language used by many politicians is vulgar. A politician who expresses himself in a thoughtful and painstaking manner is often at a disadvantage against a demagogue who makes lavish use of the most trite and commonplace notions and exploits the least noble passions. This is one of the problems with democracy.

B.   Democracy involves the quest for popular consensus, and popular consensus can also be obtained by vulgar language and behaviour.

V.   If we wanted to summarize the nature of the dangers posed by Berlusconi, we could therefore say that we are faced with a political phenomenon that brings together elements that have almost never co-existed within the same person: a concentration of the persuasive powers of the mass media, an organization with roots all over the country, and a movement held together by loyalty to its leader, who is perceived as a charismatic leader.

B.   It is undoubtedly a new phenomenon that indicates a profound malaise in our democracy.

V.   It seems to me that the creation and proliferation of personal parties to which you referred is tangible evidence that democracy has not maintained one of its promises: the one that citizens, once they have been given access to participation in public life, would become more self-aware, more sensible, more responsible and less vulnerable to the flattery of demagogues. In other words, they were supposed to be better both intellectually and morally.

After fifty years of democratic life, we have to admit reluctantly that there has been a decline and not an improvement in civic and moral values. This decline is in part related, I believe, to the end of the old parties. For all their faults, the old parties encouraged a large number of men and women to leave the home and take part in meetings. They got people used to fulfilling a few simple but significant duties: taking out a party card, paying the subscription, participating in the conference, taking part in propaganda activities, buying (or subscribing to) the newspaper, and keeping themselves informed. With the disappearance of

this kind of training ground, we find ourselves with a demagogue who has a free run of the empty streets and public
spaces, a situation I consider to be very dangerous.

Apart from demagogy, the increasingly decisive role of
money in politics is another serious threat to democracy.
Money has, in fact, become essential for winning elections
and, more generally, for creating consensus.

B.   Votes, like any other merchandise, can be bought.
This is the basic reason why money can corrupt a republic.
Those who have more money have more votes. There is a
continuing parallel between the genuine market and the
market for votes. Ideologies are also important, particularly in the case of strong ideologies, such as that of the old
Communist Party, but there can be no doubt that money
also counts. Consider the United States, where candidates
at elections first go in search of funding.

V.   In the case of the United States, scholars talk of two
electoral campaigns. The first involves the candidates canvassing for financial support, and the second canvassing for
votes. Of the two campaigns, the first is more important
than the second. The person who wins the first campaign
almost invariably wins the second. This means that pluto-
crats dominate democracies, which therefore become oli-
garchies. In an article that *La Stampa* very appropriately
entitled 'Bush de' Medici', I pointed out that in the great
and well-established American democracy, a family of
Texan magnates had managed to get two presidents
elected in the short span of twelve years, while fully ob-
serving the constitutional rules. Such enterprises were
achieved by powerful Italian families during the age of
principalities, when the Medici managed to get two family
members elected Pope in 1513 and 1523. The oligarch is
inherently dangerous, and by oligarch we mean a man who
is convinced that 'those who have wealth are very capable
of good government' and who is possessed by 'a craving for
control that tends towards both power and profit'. But the

oligarch who is also a demagogue is even more dangerous, because he knows how to win the people's favour with promises of great benefits wrapped up in 'well-chosen' words.[11]

B.   The problem you refer to is very serious. The only challenge to the power of money is the power of ideology, in the sense of a mobilizing force, as was shown by the experience of the Communist Party. Besides, the Christian Democrats, whose coffers were full because they were supported by the more affluent classes, did not rely solely on their financial muscle.

V.   The scenario you have depicted presents a stark choice between either money or ideology. You need either money, which allows you to buy consensus, or ideology, which produces activists who in turn go out to campaign for votes.

B.   In any event, money has always had an important role. Democracy operates on the basis of consensus. But how is consensus achieved? Who provides it? Theoretically, consensus should be a free choice determined on the basis of the programmes that are put forward. But is this really the case? Think of all the opportunities to manipulate consensus through dishonest manifestos. Think of the influence that the television now exercises over the great majority of people who do not read newspapers and therefore do not reflect on the various proposals presented in an article. Consider the ease with which television makes it possible to gain consensus with a few brief superficial quips. Democracy is undoubtedly still based on consensus, but it is not consensus produced by conviction freely formulated by the citizens after listening to and discussing with others. It is consensus that has been manipulated, and of this there can be no doubt.

   However, as I have explained on other occasions, democracy is not the greatest good, but the lesser evil. Things are worse in a police state. Those in power have no need of consensus; force is sufficient. If it looks for consensus, it does so through bogus elections, as occurred in communist countries where 99 per cent of the people were supposed to have voted and the result was 99 per cent in favour of the dominant party. However, they were elections.

I remember that the last elections under fascism were held in 1924 in order to vote yes or no to the 'big list'. The ballot papers for 'yes' were tricolours and you could see they were different from the outside. On this point I recall an amusing anecdote involving my dear friend Count Umberto Morra of Lavriano, who was a friend of Gobetti and a contributor to *Rivoluzione Liberale*. As he was an antifascist, he was able – lucky him – to withdraw to his beautiful ancestral country home in an area just outside Cortona. When the elections in question took place, he went to vote and the soldier on duty at the polling station came up to him and said: 'Count, you must forgive me, but I have the impression that you have voted on the wrong ballot paper.' 'No, no,' replied the count very calmly, 'that was precisely the ballot paper I wanted to vote on.'

V. When I raise the problem of the dominant role money has acquired in our political life, I know very well that it is not a new phenomenon. On this point, I think of the nature of the Medici regime in Florence during the fifteenth century. For a long time, the Medici family did not change the outward appearance of the republican institutions. Using their wealth, they distributed favours and by those favours they could rely on a vast network of friends who they placed in positions of power in the Republic. In this way, they could construct consensus and manipulate it without formally changing the institutional rules.

I brought up this example in order to emphasize that money has always had a corrupting effect in the life of free republics. But now things have got worse, because a new alliance has been created between financial power and ideological power. In Italy, Berlusconi has control of immense financial resources that can be used for creating friends and supporters. At the same time, he wields massive ideological power through the mass media. Two powers that as a rule are kept separate are today in the hands of the same man. In my opinion, this constitutes a new and disturbing situation.

B.   In Italy and elsewhere, strictly ideological power has diminished a great deal as a result of the crisis in ideologies we are all so aware of. But the presence of a candidate who possesses such immense financial resources risks altering the nature of democratic elections. They are still democratic, but Forza Italia has such an advantage in terms of resources that it is difficult to consider them democratic elections founded on freely given consensus. If Forza Italia wins the elections – and it probably will win them with the support of Fini, Bossi and Casini, who are now so very democratic, particularly in the case of Casini – we will be able to call the elections democratic in the sense that there hasn't been any vote-rigging and there hasn't been any violence or intimidation. However, no one will be able to deny the existence of hidden persuaders through television and massive posters that have covered the whole of Italy.

I wonder whether there are rules that make one democracy better than another. I am convinced that such rules can exist, but it is difficult to make sure they are observed. I fear that we will have to resign ourselves to the argument that ultimately dictatorship is worse. That is all. It is worse because either you cannot vote or you vote under duress. Of course, we are a long way away from the ideal of democracy founded on freely given consensus: one mind, one vote. It is true that parties regiment consensus after a fashion, but in spite of this, parties are indispensable. Without parties, consent would be so diffused that it would be impossible to make parliament work, as it needs political groupings. Parties compete with each other to find the best expedients for gaining consensus.

V.   What is worrying is the imbalance between the resources available to the parties.

B.   I know, but bear in mind the strength of ideologies.
The Communist Party is a good example of an ideologically powerful party, although it did have funding from the
Soviet Union and of course, the financial support of its
members.

V.   Your words remind me that the demagogue is usually
of lower-class origin, whereas now we have an oligarchic
demagogue. In *The Future of Democracy*,[12] you said that
while much has been written on the tyrant as a type, very
little has been written on the demagogue as a type. Who is
a demagogue? Someone who guides his people? Someone
who always humours the people's worst instincts? Is he an
able orator? Is he a working-class figure who has, as it
were, the gift of 'picking up' the mood of the people in a
way that no intellectual can?

B.   In practice the two figures, that of the tyrant and that
of the demagogue, become confused in the figure of the
tyrant that comes from the people. In that wonderful
description of the degeneration of the forms of government that appears in Plato's *Republic*, there is a highly
topical description of the degeneration of democracy into
demagogy.[13]

V.   Do you not get the impression that we are witnessing
precisely the degeneration of a democracy into a demagogy? Indeed into an oligarchic demagogy?

B.   This point deserves careful consideration. Berlusconi,
like the classical tyrant, believes that it is permissible for
him to do things common mortals can only dream of. A
feature of the tyrant is his belief in his power to do anything. As we have already emphasized, things go further in
his case, as he has claimed to be 'anointed by the Lord'. In

the last few days, he has even revealed that he has performed a miracle. He told the story of a sick friend whom he went to visit, and then said 'get up and walk'. Berlusconi is a man whose self-esteem is immense, a veritable superiority complex. He considers himself to be infinitely superior to other human beings. He perceives himself as an exception. How else could he have had the courage to produce all those posters? They should be counterproductive, but in his case they clearly are not.

— 8 —

Hidden Powers

V. You did not mention the danger of the demagogic oligarch in *The Future of Democracy*, and nor could you have done so without prophetic powers that would hardly suit you. You did however discuss the dangers of hidden powers. Today, we discuss this subject much less, but I don't believe that the danger has disappeared.

B. The problem of hidden powers has always tormented me. Yet it is a question that academic writing gives too little importance to. I have pointed this out to friends in the political arena on a number of occasions. Power tends to hide itself. Power increases in strength the more it is hidden from view. God is all the more powerful for being invisible. He sees and is not seen. He sees everyone and no one sees Him. Think of Bentham's *Panopticon*, the idea of a building in which the custodian in the centre can see everyone but cannot be seen. This idea of seeing without being seen is certainly symbolic of the power of God.

V. God, who sees everything without being seen, is in fact omnipotent. Infinite power corresponds to complete invisibility.

B.   The tendency of power to imitate the power of God has always existed. Consider the difference between democracy and autocracy. Democracy is an attempt to make power visible to everyone. It is or at least it should be 'power in public'. In other words, it is a form of government in which the sphere of invisible power is reduced to its absolute minimum. How could people who cannot be seen ever get elected? Autocracy cannot do without its 'secret cabinet', which is the place in which power is the least visible. Decisions have to be taken in secret, because the people must never be privy to the workings of government.

V.   Your Hobbes wrote that one of the reasons why monarchy is preferable to republican government is that in a monarchy, important decisions are taken in secret, whereas they are taken in public councils in a republic: ...

> a Monarch receiveth counsel of whom, when, and where he pleaseth; and consequently may heare the opinion of men versed in the matter about which he deliberates, of what rank or quality soever, and as long before the time of action, and with as much secrecy, as he will. But when a Soveraigne Assembly has need of Counsell, none are admitted but such as have a Right thereto from the beginning; which for the most part are of those who have beene versed more in the acquisition of Wealth than of Knowledge; and are to give their advice in long discourses, which may, and do commonly excite men to action, but not govern them in it. For the *Understanding* is by the flame of the Passions, never enlightened, but dazled: Nor is there any place, or time, wherein an Assemblie can receive Counsell with secrecie, because of their owne Multitude.[1]

This passage of Hobbes is an *inverted* confirmation of what you have been saying about invisible power. Hobbes makes the same observation, but sees things from the point of view of someone who supports monarchy: he criticizes the inability of democracy to favour the secrecy of power, which for him is a vice, and he praises the opposite tendency of the monarchy to keep power as secret as possible.

B. The decisions of the powerful must be kept secret, even though power must manifest itself in some way in order to be power. For example, there are great celebrations, triumphal arches, ostentatious pomp, and the royal coach that passes through the two wings of a crowd. Power both hides and manifests itself, so that it can attract attention and seduce the people with pomp and circumstance. It is invisible, but needs to be seen. Power instils fear through secrecy and attempts to seduce through pomp and circumstance.

Fear and deference are closely linked to the question of the secrecy of power. Power wishes to be fearful and to be respected. Fear and respect appear to be opposites, but in reality they are connected. Your Machiavelli defines Hannibal as 'venerable and terrifying'.[2] Stalin was also both feared and respected. These are the two inseparable faces of power. If you think of Stalin, the most terrifying of powerful men, you cannot deny that he was also venerable. Millions and millions of men and women venerated him around the world. Machiavelli's description of Hannibal seems perfectly suited to give an idea of power in its most perfect form: venerable and terrifying.

Both fear and veneration signify submission: one based on terror and the other on admiration. Besides, it is said that God is fearsome. The God of the Old Testament, who orders Abraham to sacrifice his son Isaac, is a fearful God, a God who instils fear. Alongside the God who instils fear, there is the God who provides consolation, bestows His blessings, is merciful and comes to people's assistance. It is to Him that they turn in difficult and desperate times. He is the God of salvation. There can be no doubt that there are these two sides to God. To continue the analogy between God and power, we can observe that God has His visible side and His invisible side.

There is the hidden side and then there is God's divine splendour, which is even compared with the sun. This should be the starting point for any attempt to understand the deep explanations for religious belief. Why do consolation and fear co-exist in religions?

V.   I do not know the answer. I have always felt a certain revulsion for the omnipotent God, and the God of dazzling splendour has always left me cold. The tendency of power to hide itself reminds me of one of Hannah Arendt's observations on totalitarianism:

> The only rule of which everybody in a totalitarian state may be sure is that the more visible government agencies are, the less power they carry, and the less is known of the existence of an institution, the more powerful it will ultimately turn out to be. According to this rule, the Soviets, recognized by a written constitution as the highest authority of the state, have less power than the Bolshevik Party; the Bolshevik Party, which recruits its members openly and is recognized as the ruling class, has less power than the secret police. Real power begins where secrecy begins.[3]

B.   Power is hidden because secrecy increases its sense of power. If power wishes to instil fear, it must reveal as little of itself as possible.

V.   However, we have to make a distinction between relations between a sovereign power and its citizens and relations between states. In the first case, the need for the transparency of power is entirely legitimate and indeed necessary for a well-functioning republic (by transparency I mean that the exercise of power can be monitored and is carried out in accordance with rules that are known and have been ratified by legislation). In international relations, on the other hand, the opposite is needed: secrecy. There are situations in which revealing the actual nature of things or allowing the enemy to see you can be extremely dangerous for the survival of the state. I would also like to examine the internal or domestic dimension to the question of secrecy and transparency. You are well aware that, concerning the terrible business of corruption, it is easier to corrupt officials and politicians when their decision-making powers are more arbitrary. The authors of an important book on political corruption wrote, 'Bribes are often accepted by individuals who hold public offices from which they exercise a kind of *discretionary power*. This discretion should be understood in the widest possible sense. Even ushers can have the power to speed up the bureaucratic process whereby documents are transferred from one department to another.'[4] Conversely, the more the conduct of politicians and officials is subject to rules and checks, the less likely they are to be corrupted:

> Transparency is indeed a fundamental element in the workings of democracy: it allows the control over government activity by citizens that is the foundation and legitimacy of representative democracy. The delegation of power by citizens to the representatives presupposes the ability of citizens to know and assess the actions of those representatives, and ultimately to hold them responsible. This applies to both elected representatives who have the task of taking political decisions, and career civil servants who have to implement those decisions.[5]

B. Greater corruption corresponds to greater secrecy. The payment of a contract that has been entered into in accordance with proper practice is made in the light of day. Money to bribe the corrupt is paid in the shadows. A legal contract is public, whereas a corrupt deal is secret. The more the corrupt feel that they are far away from prying eyes, the more they feel safe to commit unlawful acts. We have returned to the question of how power tends to conceal itself, a very important question that deserves to have more attention from political scientists, as I have already said.

Hidden Powers

V.   It would also be worth studying the relationship between hidden power and democratic life, given that the
more power is hidden, the less citizens participate in
public life. If public assemblies and self-governing bodies
do not have real power, because real power has gone
elsewhere, why should citizens take part in their activities?

B.   The fundamental principle of democracy is hostile to
secrecy. If you have to vote, you have to be able to know
about the problem on which you are expressing your
judgement and the persons who are involved.

V.   The symbols of democracy are the people in the streets
and public assemblies, although some people argue that the
symbol of modern democracy is a polling booth.

B.   Debate and voting in parliaments nearly always take
place in an open manner and citizens can attend.

V.   Always supposing that citizens want to attend. Today
the problem is not just that power tends to conceal itself;
it is also that citizens are not interested in looking. There is
widespread apathy and very little interest in following
political affairs.[6] The widespread disinterest in relation to
power and the exercise of power makes it more difficult to
challenge the tendency of power to conceal itself. If citizens are not interested in the way power is exercised,
who then should be interested? Public prosecutors? Public
prosecutors have the duty to pursue unlawful acts; citizens
have the duty to understand how and why sovereign decisions are taken. Moreover, it is unrealistic to expect public
prosecutors fully to fulfil their duty in relation to the
pursuit of unlawful acts perpetrated by politicians and
government officials without the support of public opinion or in some cases actually with hostile public opinion.

B.   Indeed, it is extremely difficult to uncover political
secrets. A recently published book that traces the history

of investigation into large-scale terrorist killings shows that those responsible were never found.[7] We never found out who threw the bomb in Piazza della Loggia in Brescia, an incident that attracted much attention. When it comes to the secret services, they are secret so that they can carry out actions that they could not carry out in full view of the public. This reminds me of the famous passage from Kant that I have quoted many times: 'All actions affecting the rights of other human beings are wrong if their maxim is not compatible with their being made public.' Kant explains this assertion very capably:

> For a maxim which I may not *declare openly* without thereby frustrating my own intention, or which must at all costs be *kept secret* if it is to succeed, or which I cannot *publicly acknowledge* without thereby inevitably arousing the resistance of everyone to my plans, can only have stirred up this necessary and general . . . opposition against me because it is itself unjust and thus constitutes a threat to everyone.[8]

The premise to Kant's argument is clear: 'Keeping secret an intention, a pact or, if it were possible, a public provision, is in itself proof of unlawfulness.'

V.   Kant means that in order to be legitimate, power must justify its actions publicly.

B.   If it cannot do so, this means that the action is unlawful. For example, could a state openly declare its intention to spark off a war of conquest?

V.   You have yourself observed that public power must be subject to scrutiny for the principle of open government to be enacted by politicians rather than just proclaimed by philosophers, and you add that the form of government in which such scrutiny can take place is democracy. I would specify uncorrupted democracy, in which citizens have a modicum of civic awareness that gives them the motivation and courage to scrutinize public decisions and criticize them, and to expose abuses of power and unlawful acts. Democracy is not enough to counter the tendency of power to conceal itself and therefore to become arbitrary. You need a citizens' democracy in which people are not only citizens in name but also have the mentality of citizens. We should not forget that one of the principal features of political power is its skill in pretence and concealment.[9]

B. The arts of dissembling and lying are also founded on ways of concealing oneself. You can hide yourself by wearing a mask or by lying. By wearing a mask or lying you display something that is not yourself. You wear a mask because you do not want to be seen. This theme of the mask is a very interesting one. Consider, for example, Verdi's famous opera *Un ballo in maschera* (*A Masked Ball*), in which a crime takes place between people who are dancing with masks.

— 9 —

Can the Republic be Renewed?

V.   We have discussed the Italian Republic's ills, and we have dwelled upon the crisis of political parties, the proliferation of personal parties, the danger of the demagogic oligarch, the increasingly dominant role of wealth and the risks posed by hidden powers. Perhaps it would be useful to discuss some possible remedies. As you know, many think that the best cure for the Republic's ills and particularly unstable government would be institutional reform. Some people even think that we need to set up another constituent assembly.

B.   I have always been involved in political theory, but I have never dealt with political engineering. If you asked me, 'Is it better to have a parliamentary republic, a presidential republic or a semi-presidential republic?', I would not know what to reply. I am full of doubts. These are problems that I debate within my head without ever arriving at a clear opinion. Is proportional representation better than first-past-the-post? Is it better to have one chamber or two?

V.   I have always been struck by your silence on arguments that everyone has been heatedly debating for years.

Can the Republic be Renewed?

Everybody appears to have the recipe for saving us all from the failings of the Republic.

B.   The only thing I have always said is that I have serious doubts about the usefulness of constitutional reform. I have doubts over whether it should be done or not, and whether it should be done by referendum or by constituent assembly. As my ideas are not clear on the subject, I would prefer not to discuss them, in spite of being constantly urged to do so. But I do not see the need for constitutional reform. The idea of a great reform was launched by Craxi.[1] There have been several parliamentary commissions, the last of which was chaired by D'Alema. A great mass of paper has been consumed and weighs down the shelves of the state archive, but nothing has ever come of it. Nothing, absolutely nothing. One proposal contradicted the other.

V.   My position is that constituent assemblies are necessary when there are exceptional reasons for convening them, such as the collapse of a regime, a revolution or a war that has been lost. In these circumstances it is necessary to commence a process of reform to redefine where sovereignty lies and therefore to revise the legal system. It does not appear to me that in Italy we face a crisis of such magnitude as to make it necessary to introduce constitutional reform. The political parties of the so-called First Republic have disappeared or changed name, and new parties have been created. The composition of the Parliament and various regional, provincial and local councils has changed, but the sovereign power remains unchanged.

B.   I could not agree more. And then you have to consider what kind of constituent assembly would be produced by our current mediocre political elite. A constituent assembly requires great personalities, like the ones we had in the Constituent Assembly of 1946. On the other hand, it is also true that it is very difficult to reform the Constitution through the procedures provided for in the current

Constitution. Article 138 lays down that laws revising the Constitution and other constitutional laws must be adopted by each chamber 'with two successive decisions separated by a period of not less than three months, and must be approved by an absolute majority of the members of each chamber in the second vote'. It is unthinkable that constitutional reform could be introduced with the current Parliament. Italy is undergoing a very serious historical crisis. It is suffering from a chronic disease – probably not a fatal one, but certainly chronic – in the sense that it has been dragging on for a long time and no end appears to be in sight. As I have already said, one of the symptoms of this disease is the constant formation of new parties. What is the purpose of these new parties? What do their founders wish to gain?

V.   When you mentioned the great political and intellectual qualities of the constituent assemblies of 1946, I was reminded of the words of Guglielmo Negri, whom we have now sadly lost. He once told me – I cannot remember exactly when – that the constituent assemblies of 1946 were politically and ideologically divided but had behind them a shared experience of suffering and humiliation, first experienced under fascism and then during the Second World War. The tragic experience they shared was an important reason to look together for an institutional structure that offered the best possible guarantees to prevent Italy living through another tragedy similar to the one they had just experienced. In other words, they had a sense of common purpose. They had different ideas about the future, but they perceived the past in the same way: never again did they want to see fascism, and never again did they want to have a monarchy. Today, any constituent assemblies would lack that sense of common purpose. This is why I believe it completely inappropriate to start talking about a constituent assembly.

B.   The parties that made up the Constituent Assembly had come through the experience of the Resistance. The

Communist Party, which had been the principal force in the Resistance, played a key role in the Assembly. The Communist Party voted for a liberal and democratic constitution that also included social rights, while not demanding anything in exchange to satisfy its ideology at the time. This backs up what you were just saying: namely that the communists had also just come through the experience of fighting fascism. Antifascism was the thing that united them. I say this now to point out that there could never be a constituent assembly while Berlusconi is saying that it is a moral duty to fight communism, and for him communists include everyone but himself and his allies.

V.   Today there are no longer any shared ideals that could unite a constituent assembly, should one be set up. In a situation of this kind, a new constitution would be impossible, unless there was a demiurge, a legislator who provides a ready-made constitution, such as the one referred to by Rousseau in *The Social Contract*.[2] But Rousseau's Legislator is a myth.

B.   The problem is that we have gone from antifascism to anticommunism. If it were up to Berlusconi, the new constitution would be an anticommunist one. Of course you understand that anticommunism today is a much weaker force than antifascism then. However, if you talk about antifascism now, it seems that you are saying something anachronistic that no longer has any sense, value or reason for existing. Half a century has passed, and people have forgotten.

V.   We may well run the risk of sounding anachronistic, but it is a risk I am very happy to run. Indeed, I would consider it a compliment to be thought of as anachronistic. As far as I am concerned, the conflict between fascism and antifascism is more of a moral conflict than a political one. Fascism and antifascism are two irreconcilable philosophies of life based on opposing moral principles. Auschwitz is the dividing line. Those with a fascist mentality believe Auschwitz to be something exaggerated by communists, a deplorable excess or even a glorious episode. Antifascists consider it to be the most repugnant atrocity that to date humanity has been able to think up. Being antifascist means an incontestable condemnation of the death camp without any provisos or appeals to mitigating circumstances, and this condemnation leads to another equally incontestable condemnation of everything that made the death camp possible: nationalism, racism, totalitarianism and fanatical identification with a leader who is capable of anything. Fascism as a culture and way of life still exists. You can see it in the way many people talk about those who are different, the weak and women. Even if it means being in a tiny minority and even if it means being the object of derision, it is my opinion that the contrast between fascism and antifascism must be kept solid. Indeed, I believe that it needs to be reinforced.

B. Fini,[3] who loves to proclaim his democratic credentials, is surrounded by men who despise democracy and the rule of law, and who perceive politics as a decisive and head-on confrontation. Berlusconi, with his anticommunism, also bears a considerable responsibility for this situation. Anticommunism accommodates fascism; antifascism accommodates communism. In such a context, it seems entirely inappropriate to be thinking about a constituent assembly.

V. Is there anything in our constitution that prevents us from dealing with Italy's fundamental problems, starting with the question of the decline in the rule of law? In my opinion, there is nothing in our constitution that impedes us from finding solutions to our problems. The problem is more to do with the poor quality of our political class or rather our political elite. I fully realize that democrats are suspicious of the word 'elite', because the theory of elites came about as a conservative response to the gains being

made by democracy. There are however democratic political writers who have developed theories that express the
need to create new elites capable of resolving Italy's historical ills. Given that constitutional reform cannot be the
way to deal with the Republic's difficulties, would it not
be better to give thought to how we can develop a new
democratic elite?

B.   It is difficult to form an elite. You can reform the
Constitution or you can introduce new law, but how can
you renew the ruling class? There either is or isn't a ruling
class. I remember a famous article by Guido Dorso that
spoke of 'the mystery of the ruling class'.[4] The problem is
that there is no ruling class that can be taken seriously in
Italy today. The mystery of the elites for Dorso was that in
some periods an elite is formed while in others it isn't.
Wasn't the elite that carried through the Risorgimento a
genuine elite? Even in the First Republic, Christian Democracy was an elite party compared with Forza Italia or
Alleanza Nazionale, in spite of all the criticisms we could
direct against it. It was a party that had personalities like
De Gasperi, Moro, Fanfani and Zaccagnini. We no longer
have leaders of this kind. There has been a decline.

V.   It is difficult to envisage a civic rebirth of our Republic without the creation of a new political elite.

B.   But how and where would this elite come from? The
personalities that emerge from time to time are one worse
than the other, even within the left. The Republican Party,
for example, constituted a genuine elite at the time of Ugo
La Malfa; now it has a very marginal role.

V.   Even the Action Party has been accused of being an
elite party.

B.   Elite parties struggle to survive in a democracy. At the
first elections, the Action Party did not win a single seat, as

I remember very well because it was the only election campaign I ever took part in – the one in 1946 for the Constituent Assembly. It gained seven members of parliament from what under that electoral law were called the 'leftovers'. Seven members of parliament as against 104 for the Communist Party and 207 for the Christian Democrats. Just think what such an experience meant to a person like me who was only then getting involved in political life (in 1945 I was thirty-six years old) and discovered that politically his party counted for nothing. The Action Party was an elite party and that is why it never came to anything, even though it had a leading role in the partisan war alongside the Communist Party.

V.   You bemoan the fact that the Action Party had very little electoral weight, but you cannot deny that it had enormous influence in terms of politics and ideals. This is demonstrated by the fact that even its critics admit that the Action Party provided intellectual and political leadership. Now there isn't even that.

B.   The Action Party was a party of intellectuals. It was a party that had various components that ranged from a leftward-leaning right to a genuinely left-wing current. There were philo-socialists like Foa, but also people like Omodeo, Salvatorelli and De Ruggiero, who were leftish liberals. In the middle there was La Malfa. You know very well how the split occurred at the first congress. The Action Party met before the Constituent Assembly for its first congress and divided in two. This was a party that was already small before the elections for the Constituent Assembly. The result was seven deputies for the Action Party and two for the Republican Alliance. The Christian Democrats triumphed thanks to their deep roots in Italian society and the support of the Catholic Church. There were parishes in every town, but there weren't Action Party branches. A party of intellectuals can only be a minority party.

V.   It may have been a party of intellectuals, but I believe it is hard to deny that its members played an important role in encouraging the development of democracy in Italy and particularly in encouraging the democratic trend within the Communist Party. And yet members of the Action Party, particularly those in Turin, have been fiercely criticized for being more antifascist than anticommunist, and therefore not equally distanced from both fascists and communists.[5]

I find this criticism weak in both historical and logical terms. It is weak in historical terms because Action Party members, whether in Turin or elsewhere, considered liberal-democratic principles to be completely essential to any policy of social renewal. Carlo Rosselli's writings clearly demonstrate this during the period of Giustizia e Libertà.[6] 'The communist revolution in relation to fascism', he wrote in an article of 1936, 'would only be half a revolution: in some ways it would prolong its dictatorial forms and mentality, while failing to tackle the problems of freedom and morality whose importance fascism has further highlighted.'[7] That same year, he wrote on the Russian communists' position on the war: 'We should not overlook the extremely grave consequences that the USSR's position will have on the international labour movement and the communist parties, which will be sacrificed in the case of war.'[8] A few months later, in an article entitled 'Reflections on the state and party', he revealed the limitations of the Russian experience with a clear reference to the liberal principle of free competition between people, organizations and ideas:

> The best defence against the arrogance of ruling classes is freedom to criticize and actual competition or the constant opportunity to engage in it. If the Communist Party in Russia were to compete with other proletarian parties or even only grant genuine freedom of discussion within the party, you could be sure that they would have abandoned centralism long ago and renewed their ruling caste. The

task of a socialist society is not to destroy competition between people and organizations, but to make that competition truly effective and free.[9]

Finally – in order not to overdo the quotations – he pointed out when writing about the Church, 'religious societies certainly do not have a monopoly on certain forms of intolerance, persecution and authoritarianism. We can see that the cult of the Proletariat, the Race or the Nation have led to the same results in Russia, Germany and Italy, but without the same mitigating circumstances.'[10]

The weakness in the argument that I am examining is that members of the Action Party entered into a critical dialogue with Italian communists, and this did not involve any ambiguity in their liberal-democratic position, but was in fact entirely consistent with such a position, particularly in Italy. This was for the obvious reason that in Italy liberal democracy could only be achieved and was in fact achieved by acting *against* fascism and *in concert with* the Italian Communist Party. To create a liberal democracy in Italy it was necessary to fight the fascist regime as an absolute evil in order to destroy it, and to maintain a favourable relationship with Italian communists so as to help them accept liberal and democratic principles. The Action Party was the only political formation that could have achieved both these tasks. And they did achieve them with great distinction, much to the benefit of liberal democracy.

Besides, this intransigence with fascists and openness to dialogue with Italian communists was shared by Ugo La Malfa, a member of the Action Party who did not come from Turin. No one in their right mind would have accused him of being uncertain about his support for liberal democracy. Ugo La Malfa behaved exactly like the much maligned Action Party members in Turin: he entered into debates with Italian communists, which could become fierce polemics, but he was not on speaking terms with

Almirante and his thugs.[11] He acted in that manner not *in spite of* being a democratic liberal, but precisely *because* he was one. The Action Party's lack of equidistance between communism and fascism, particularly in the Turin branch, is therefore a virtue and not a vice, especially in the current situation in which fascism is still a real problem and communism is a threat that only exists in Berlusconi's imagination. While it is commendable to be an antifascist, it is a mark of even greater virtue to be an intransigent antifascist. Or at least it's better than being a luke-warm antifascist? More generally, isn't it more praise-worthy to defend the noble political and idealistic principles with intransigence in a country that for centuries has been dominated by unprincipled cynics and masters of accommodations and compromises? The problem in Italy is that there have always been too few people who have inter-preted and practised politics in this manner.

I have dwelled upon the Action Party's legacy because I do not believe that we can afford to ignore this political tradition and its ideas. Indeed, I am convinced that the right way towards the rebirth of Italian society is through the synthesis of the liberal-socialist tradition and the republican tradition that was achieved in the Action Party, but unfor-tunately for too short a time. Liberal socialism and repub-licanism need each other. Liberal socialism upholds the tradition of social emancipation, but lacks a genuine under-standing of the significance of the state. For very good reasons, it has always been anti-statist.[12] An understanding of the significance of the state or rather the public good, seen as the primary duty of politicians and citizens, has always been the distinctive intellectual and political elem-ent in republicanism. I do not know whether a political force inspired by liberal socialism and backed by republican awareness of the state could ever be created in Italy, even on a small scale, but if it did ever occur, it would certainly make an important contribution to resolving Italy's ills. Even President Ciampi suggested that he was working in this direction when he visited the Domus Mazziniana in Pisa and paid homage to the place that commemorates Mazzini and the Rosselli brothers.

B.   Ciampi is a man who knows what he is doing, and who has reassessed the meaning of patriotism in a simple and unpretentious manner. Ciampi represents Italy and does an excellent job. He is a capable, intelligent and cultured man. I have to say that he is our only hope. We have generally been lucky with our Presidents of the Republic. We have had Pertini, Scalfaro and now Ciampi. Like any decent person, he does not dissemble. He also has this idea that he has to represent Italy. There can be no doubt that Ciampi is an important reference point. Ciampi is a good representative of antifascism, which is now more important than ever. Ciampi was a student of Calogero, who was one of the great masters of antifascism. However, the problem of the elite remains, and I don't know how we could form a new elite.

V.   I do not underestimate the difficulties of such an undertaking, but I believe that the reconstruction of a democratic elite is a worthwhile enterprise. I understand your pessimism, but I would like to think that Machiavelli was right when he wrote that Italy 'appears to have been created to resurrect the past'.

Notes

CHAPTER 1 VIRTUE AND THE REPUBLIC

1 See Philip Pettit, *Republicanism. A Theory of Freedom and Government* (Oxford: Oxford University Press, 1977), and Quentin Skinner, *Liberty before Liberalism* (Cambridge: Cambridge University Press, 1998).

2 Norberto Bobbio, *Teoria generale della politica*, ed. Michelangelo Bovero (Turin: Einaudi, 1999).

3 Jean-Jacques Rousseau, *The Social Contract*, in *The Social Contract and Discourses*, trans. G. D. H. Cole (London, Melbourne and Toronto: Everyman, 1979), pp. 192–3. For the original French, see *Du contrat social*, in *Oeuvres complètes*, ed. Bernard Gagnebin and Marcel Raymond (Paris: Gallimard, 1964), vol. III, pp. 379–80.

4 Carlo Cattaneo, 'La città considerata come principio ideale delle istorie italiane', in *Opere scelte*, ed. Delia Castelnuovo Frigessi (Turin: Einaudi, 1972), vol. IV, p. 123.

5 Umberto Bossi is the leader of the Lega Nord ('Northern League') [*Translator's note*].

6 Maurizio Viroli, *Dalla politica alla ragion di stato* (Rome: Donzelli, 1994).

7 The quote from Machiavelli is taken from *Discursus florentinarum rerum post mortem iunioris Laurentii Medices*, in *Opere*, ed. Corrado Vivanti (Turin: Einaudi-Gallimard, 1997), p. 745.

8 Norberto Bobbio, 'Istituzioni e costituzione democratica', in *Giustizia e Libertà*, the daily newspaper of the Action Party, 6 November 1945; now in *Tra due repubbliche*, ed. Tommaso Greco (Rome: Donzelli, 1996), pp. 31–3.

CHAPTER 2   PATRIOTISM

1 Carlo Rosselli, *Socialismo liberale* (Turin: Einaudi, 1979), p. 135.
2 Carlo Rosselli, 'La lezione della Sarre', in *Scritti dell'esilio* (Turin: Einaudi, 1992), vol. II, p. 96; and 'Discussione sul Risorgimento', in *Scritti dell'esilio*, pp. 154–5.
3 Carlo Rosselli, 'Irredentismo slavo', in *Scritti dell'esilio*, pp. 46–9.
4 Carlo Rosselli, 'Opposizione d'attacco', in *Scritti dell'esilio*, p. 233.
5 Carlo Rosselli, 'Fronte verso l'Italia', in *Scritti dell'esilio*, p. 4.
6 Mazzini, Garibaldi and Pisacane were three leading figures in the Italian Risorgimento or campaign for unification. Mazzini was a strict republican and refused to participate with the Kingdom of Italy unified under the House of Savoy. Garibaldi, the most famous of the Risorgimento figures and something of a hero in Victorian Britain, had what can only be described as an adventurous life involving armed struggles in Latin America and Italy. The popular uprising he triggered in Sicily with just 1,000 men was the great political and military success that led to the creation of the Kingdom of Italy. All the men were radicals of the left, but Pisacane had the most consistently socialist beliefs. In 1857, his landing in the South was as disastrous as Garibaldi's was successful. He and 300 others lost their lives [*translator's note*].
7 Carlo Rosselli, 'Realismo', in *Scritti dell'esilio*, p. 341.
8 Piero Calamandrei, *Diario 1939–1945*, ed. Aldo Agosti (Florence: La Nuova Italia, 1982), vol. II, p. 155.
9 Piero Gobetti was a radical liberal thinker who much influenced the development of the antifascist movement in Italy, in spite of dying very young in 1926. Giovanni Gentile was a philosopher and keen supporter of Mussolini's regime. He remained loyal to the nazi-fascist puppet state, the Republic of Salò, and was killed by Partisans in 1944 [*translator's note*].

10   Carlo Cattaneo, *Scritti politici ed epistolario*, ed. Gabriele Rosa and Jessie White Mario (Florence: Barbera, 1894), vol. I, p. 263.

11   Gian Enrico Rusconi is an Italian academic whose book, *Se cessiamo di essere una nazione* (Bologna: Il Mulino, 1993), discusses questions of nation and identity [*translator's note*].

12   Quentin Skinner, 'Ambrogio Lorenzetti: The artist as political philosopher', in *Proceedings of the British Academy*, 72 (1986), pp. 1–56.

13   Carlo Cattaneo (1801–1869) is another lesser-known Risorgimento figure. It is Bobbio's belief that his lack of nationalistic rhetoric and his preference for a federal regime meant that he has been undeservedly ignored. Carlo Rosselli was one of the most important antifascist figures before the Second World War. He and Emilio Lussu founded the organization Giustizia e Libertà, which in spite of many setbacks remained the most effective antifascist force in the thirties. He was killed with his brother Nello by French fascists of La Cagoule on specific orders from Mussolini's regime [*translator's note*].

14   Renato Guttuso (1911–1987), Italian artist and antifascist [*translator's note*].

CHAPTER 3   WHAT KIND OF FREEDOM?

1   Philip Pettit, *Republicanism. A Theory of Freedom and Government* (Oxford: Oxford University Press, 1977). See also Quentin Skinner, *Liberty before Liberalism* (Cambridge: Cambridge University Press, 1998).

2   See Norberto Bobbio, *The Future of Democracy*, trans. R. Bellany (Cambridge: Polity, 1987); original title: *Il futuro della democrazia* (Rome–Bari: Laterza, 1984) [*Translator's note*].

3   Norberto Bobbio, *Politica e cultura* (Turin: Einaudi, 1974; 1st edn, 1955), pp. 172–4.

CHAPTER 4   MEEKNESS AND INTRANSIGENCE

1   Norberto Bobbio, *In Praise of Meekness*, trans. Teresa Chataway (Cambridge: Polity, 2000); original title: *Elogio della mitezza e altri scritti morali* (Milan: Nuova Pratiche Editrice, 1998).
2   Lega Nord (or Northern League) is a regional party with secessionist tendencies and a strongly xenophobic political culture [*translator's note*].
3   Edgardo Sogno, the so-called 'anticommunist partisan', died in 2000 and was given a state funeral by the centre-left government. This decision caused a great deal of controversy as Sogno revealed in 1977 that he had been involved in the plots to stage a coup and introduce a 'strong government' and more recently had argued for the destruction of the democratic state [*translator's note*].
4   Francesco Guicciardini, *Ricordi*, series B, n. 14.
5   Niccolò Machiavelli, *Discourses on the First Ten of Livy's Books*. For the original Italian, see *Discorsi sopra la prima deca di Tito Livio*, in *Tutte le opere* (Florence: Sansoni, 1971), I.12, p. 96.

CHAPTER 5   RIGHTS AND DUTIES

1   Norberto Bobbio, *The Age of Rights*, trans. Allan Cameron (Cambridge: Polity, 1996); original title: *L'età dei diritti* (Turin: Einaudi, 1990).
2   Maurizio Viroli, *Repubblicanesimo* (Rome–Bari: Laterza, 1999).
3   Samuel Pufendorf, *De officio hominis et civis juxta legem naturalem libri duo* (Lund: 1673), I. iv.1.
4   Ibid., I. v. 1.
5   Ibid., I. vi. 1.
6   Quoted in *Grande dizionario della lingua italiana* (Turin: UTET, 1966), vol. IV, p. 989. Francesco De Sanctis (1817–1883) was the most famous Italian literary critic of the nineteenth century and author of *The History of Italian Literature*. He also wrote some minor compositions of his own and

participated in the 1848 uprising in Naples, for which he was imprisoned. With unification, he started a political career and was for a short while the Minister of Education [*translator's note*].

7   Alessandro Passerin d'Entrèves, 'Intorno all'obbligo politico', in *Rivista di Filosofia*, LVII (1966), pp. 156–64.

8   Sergio D'Antoni, a former trade-union leader, set up a new party called European Democracy [Democrazia Europea]. Mastella is the leader of Udeur, one of the many new political formations in Italy [*translator's note*].

CHAPTER 6   FEAR OF GOD AND LOVE OF GOD

1   John 3: 36.

2   Niccolò Machiavelli, *Discourses on the First Ten of Livy's Book's*. For the original Italian, see *Discorsi sopra la prima deca di Tito Livio*, in *Tutte le opere* (Florence: Sansoni, 1971), II.2.

3   Ibid., I. 11.

4   Alexis de Tocqueville, *Democracy in America*, vol. I, XVII, 5 (London: Everyman's Library, 1994) p. 303: 'Society has no future life to hope for or to fear; and provided the citizens profess a religion, the peculiar tenets of that religion are of little importance to its interests.'

5   Ibid., vol. I, I, 5, p. 22.

6   Ibid., vol. I, XVII, 5, p. 307.

7   Cesare Beccaria, *Dei delitti e delle pene*, ed. Piero Calamandrei (Florence: Le Monnier, 1945), ch. XX.

8   Montesquieu, *The Spirit of the Laws*, XXVI.2.

9   Thomas Hobbes, *Leviathan* (London: Penguin, 1985), XIV, p. 189.

10   Tocqueville, *Democracy in America*, vol. I, ch. XIV, sect. 4, pp. 247–8.

11   *Il sorpasso* was directed by Dino Risi in 1962, a comedy in the neo-realist tradition [*translator's note*].

12   Walter Veltroni is a leading figure in the Democratic Party of the Left (the former Communists) [*translator's note*].

13 Norberto Bobbio, *Left and Right*, trans. and introduction by Allan Cameron (Cambridge: Polity, 1996); original title: *Destra e sinistra* (Rome: Donzelli, 1995, 2nd edn).

14 Saint Josephy Benedict Cottolengo founded, amongst other associations, the Congregation of the Priests of the Holy Trinity to run homes for epileptics, the deaf and dumb, orphans, old people, and the mentally ill [*translator's note*].

15 Giuseppe Mazzini, 'Dal Concilio a Dio', in *Scritti editi e inediti* (Imola: Galeati, 1906–), vol LXXXVI, p. 241.

16 See Maurizio Viroli, *Per amore della patria* (Rome–Bari: Laterza, 1995), pp. 23–7.

17 'If any man come to me and hate not his father, and mother, and wife, and children, and brethren, and sisters, yea, and his own life also, he cannot be my disciple' (Luke 14: 26).

18 Norberto Bobbio, 'Religione e religiosità', *Micromega*, 2 (2000).

19 'Cattolici e laici ex nemici', *La Repubblica*, 22 November 2000.

20 See Norberto Bobbio, *Old Age and Other Essays*, trans. Allan Cameron (Cambridge: Polity, 2002); original title: *De senectute* (Turin: Einaudi, 1996), pp. 35–41.

CHAPTER 7 THE REPUBLIC AND ITS PROBLEMS

1 Forza Italia is the party founded by the entrepreneur and media mogul Silvio Berlusconi. Its name is primarily associated with the slogan shouted from the terraces in support of the national football team: 'Come on, Italy', but through the word *Forza* ('strength', 'force') and *Italia*, it invites connotations of nationalism and strong government. Bobbio famously attacked Forza Italia for having a leader even before it had been constituted as a party; see N. Bobbio, *A Political Life*, trans. Allan Cameron (Cambridge: Polity, 2002) pp. 157–8 [*translator's note*].

2 Letter from Francesco Guicciardini to Niccolò Machiavelli, of 18 May 1521, in Niccolò Machiavelli, *Opere*, ed. Franco Gaeta (Turin: UTET, 1984), vol. III, p. 525. Francesco

Guicciardini (1483–1540), Italian aristocrat, politician, political thinker and historian, is often contrasted with Machiavelli, but in many ways their views were the product of both the well-established humanist tradition and the political vicissitudes of their native city, Florence [*translator's note*].

3　Robert Michels, Political Parties: A Sociological Study of the Oligarchical Tendencies of Modern Democracy (1912); (New York: Dover publications, n.d.)

4　Il Polo delle Libertà: 'The Focus of Freedoms'. This is rightwing electoral alliance that consists of Berlusconi's Forza Italia, Alleanza Nazionale ('ex'-fascists), and the Lega Nord (a xenophobic regional party that demands the secession of the North with varying degrees of conviction) [*translator's note*].

5　Luigi Einaudi (1874–1961), an economist and statesman, became the first President of the Republic of Italy in 1948 and remained in office for one seven-year term [*translator's note*].

6　Berlinguer, Nenni and La Malfa were leaders for many years of the Communist Party, the Socialist Party and the Republican Party respectively [*translator's note*].

7　See Max Weber, *Wirtschaft und Gesellschaft*, Eng. trans. *Economy and Society*, 2vols. (Berkeley: University of California Press, 1978) Book IV, Section V.

8　Martin Luther King, *The Strength of Love* (New York: Harper and Row, 1963).

9　'I do not want to judge whether he [Savonarola] was right or wrong, because one must always speak with reverence of so great a man, but I can indeed confirm that very many people believed him without having seen anything out of the ordinary to make them believe him, because his life, his doctrine and the questions he championed were sufficient to make people have faith in him,' in Machiavelli, *Discourses*, II.2.

10　For the distinction between oligarch and demagogue, see Michelangelo Bovero, *Contro il governo dei peggiori* (Rome–Bari: Laterza, 2000), pp. 127–39.

11　Ibid., pp. 135–6.

12　Norberto Bobbio, *The Future of Democracy*, trans. R. Bellamy (Cambridge: Polity, 1987); original title: *Il futuro della democrazia* (Rome–Bari: Laterza, 1984).

13　Plato, *The Republic*, pp. 562–4.

CHAPTER 8 HIDDEN POWERS

1   Thomas Hobbes, *Leviathan*, (1651), ch. 19, p. 96 (London: Penguin Classics, 1985), p. 242.
2   'This could only have arisen from his inhuman cruelty which, together with his infinite virtues, meant that to his soldiers he was always both venerable and terrifying'; in Niccolò Machiavelli, *The Prince*, XVII (London: Penguin Books, 1961), p. 97.
3   Hannah Arendt, *The Origins of Totalitarianism* (1951; San Diego and New York: Harcourt, n.d.), p. 403.
4   Donatella della Porta and Aberto Vannucci, *Un paese anormale. Come la classe politica ha perso l'occasione di Mani Pulite* (Rome–Bari: Laterza, 1999), p. 92.
5   Ibid., p. 91.
6   On the decline in the participation of citizens in political and social life in the United States, see Robert Putnam, *Bowling Alone: The Collapse and Revival of American Community* (New York: Simon & Schuster, 2000).
7   'The scourge [of Italy's troubled history] is perhaps to be found precisely in this concept of "secrecy" which transformed itself over time from its initial state, a more or less physiological one in any democracy, into a veritable cancer. *Secrecy* ultimately fed upon itself and corrupted the very fabric of the state'; in Giovanni Fasanella and Claudio Sestrieri, *Segreto di stato* (Turin: Einaudi, 2000), p. VIII.
8   Immanuel Kant, *Perpetual Peace. A Philosophical Sketch* (1795), in Kant, *Political Writings* (Cambridge: CUP, 1991), p. 126. See also Norberto Bobbio, *Teoria generale della politica* (Turin: Einaudi, 1999), p. 361.
9   'But one must know how to colour one's actions and to be a great liar and deceiver. Men are so simple, and so much creatures of circumstance, that the deceiver will always find someone ready to be deceived'; in Niccolò Machiavelli, *The Prince*, trans. George Bull (London: Penguin Books, 1975), p. 100.

CHAPTER 9   CAN THE REPUBLIC BE RENEWED?

1   Bettino Craxi (1934–2000), who was leader of the Socialist Party from 1976 to 1993 and Prime Minister from 1983 to 1987, died in disgrace in Tunisia unable to return to Italy because of outstanding convictions for corruption [*translator's note*].

2   Jean-Jacques Rousseau, *The Social Contract*, ch. VII, 'The Legislator', in *The Social Contract and Discourses*, trans. G. D. H. Cole (London, Melbourne and Toronto: Everyman's Library, 1973), pp. 194–7.

3   Gianfranco Fini: the leader of Alleanza Nazionale, the 'ex-fascist' party which is currently part of the ruling coalition that came to power in 2001 [*translator's note*].

4   'The formation of a ruling class is a historical mystery that neither materialism nor idealism have succeeded in explaining'; in Guido Dorso, 'Dittatura, classe politica e classe dirigente', in *Opere*, ed. Carlo Muscetta (Turin: Einaudi, 1949), vol. II, p. 9.

5   Ernesto Galli della Loggia, 'La democrazia immaginaria dell'azionismo', in *Il Mulino*, XLII (1993), pp. 260–1.

6   Giustizia e Libertà: the most important antifascist organization in the thirties, which was led by Carlo Rosselli and Emilio Lussu. It united with other forces to form the Action Party, but the name continued as the title of the Action Party's newspaper.

7   See the celebrated article by Carlo Rosselli in *Scritti dell'esilio*, ed. Costanzo Casucci (Turin: Einaudi, 1992), vol. II, p. 296.

8   Ibid., p. 329.

9   Carlo Rosselli, 'Tesi sullo stato e il partito', in *Scritti dell'esilio*, p. 367.

10 Rosselli, *Scritti dell'esilio*, p. 567.

11 See Ugo La Malfa, *Discutendo di sinistra*, ed. Adolfo Battaglia (Rome: Editori Riuniti, 1999). Giorgio Almirante (1914–1988) led the neo-fascist Italian Social Movement for many years and had held high office in the nazi-fascist Italian Social Republic (of Salò) [*translator's note*].

12 See the famous article by Carlo Rosselli, 'Contro lo stato', in *Scritti dell'esilio*, vol. II, pp. 42–5.